DISCOVER YOUR SCOTTISH ANCESTRY

DISCOVER YOUR SCOTTISH ANCESTRY

Internet and Traditional Resources

Graham S. Holton and Jack Winch

A Roberts Rinehart Book

TAYLOR TRADE PUBLISHING
Lanham • New York • Dallas • Boulder • Toronto • Oxford

The authors would like to thank Mr. David Brown and other staff
of the National Archives of Scotland for reading and commenting
on sections of the text.

Originally published in Great Britain by Edinburgh University
Press Ltd., 22 George Square, Edinburgh.

Roberts Rinehart Publishers
A Member of The Rowman & Littlefield Publishing Group, Inc.
4501 Forbes Boulevard, Suite 200
Lanham, MD 20706

Distributed by National Book Network

Library of Congress Cataloging-in-Publication Data

Holton, Graham S.
   Discover your Scottish ancestry : Internet and traditional resources /
Graham S. Holton and Jack Winch.
      p. cm.
"A Roberts Rinehart book"
   ISBN 1-57098-428-X (pbk. : alk. paper)
   1. Scottish Americans—Genealogy—Handbooks, manuals, etc.
2. United States—Genealogy—Handbooks, manuals, etc. 3.
Scotland—Genealogy—Handbooks, manuals, etc. I. Winch, Jack.
II. Title.
   E184.S3H65 2004
      929'.1'0899163073—dc22
                                                                2003023534

⊗™ The paper used in this publication meets the minimum
requirements of American National Standard for Information
Sciences—Permanence of Paper for Printed Library Materials,
ANSI/NISO Z39.48-1992.

Manufactured in the United States of America.

CONTENTS

FIGURES

FOREWORD

It is now six years since the publication of our first book on Scottish family history, *My Ain Folk*. During this period the Internet has become firmly established as part of everyday life. Family history has in its turn become established as one of the most popular subjects on the Internet. Many family historians today find the use of e-mail and the Web to be an indispensable aid in their researches.

The Internet is a continually changing landscape which we have attempted to chart at the time of publication, highlighting what we believe to be its most significant and useful features.

The list of Web sites included in this book is as up to date as possible at the time of printing, but readers can refer to the University of Strathclyde Library's Scottish family history Web pages for the most up to date listing of many of these sites.

Perhaps the other main development has been in the field of genetics as applied to genealogy and we have also included a section dealing with this subject. Amongst other additions, there are sections dealing with the storage and preservation of documents and the interpretation of older styles of handwriting.

As in our previous book, we aim to appeal to both beginners and those who already have some experience of family history research. Although technology has recently had a major impact on family history, the traditional methods and principles of research still form the essential core of this fascinating subject. We hope that our advice will give you a good grounding in these methods and principles and that the bibliography and list of Web sites will allow you to investigate more fully any particular areas of interest.

INTRODUCTION

'Why, oh why, do I want to research my family history?' Have you ever stopped to think?

You may only have a hazy idea of your motives, or you may have some very specific reason for embarking on this family history business.

Maybe it is purely for the fun of it; of discovering your 'roots', delving into the unknown. Where were your ancestors born, where did they live, what were their occupations and what sort of lives did they lead? You may well, as many families do, have a family tradition which says that a particular relative was present at some historic event, or even left an unclaimed fortune. Such stories have perhaps spurred you into action, in an attempt to prove their truth or otherwise. Despite natural scepticism, there is very often a grain of truth in such traditions but at the same time they are not usually 'the whole truth'.

FAMILY TRADITIONS

Here is one amongst several stories in one of the author Graham Holton's families, part of which has been proven by means of several sources. According to family legend a McArthur ancestor was a ship's surgeon aboard the *Victory* at the Battle of Trafalgar in 1805.

After some work, the author's descent from a Florence McArthur in Glasgow was traced and some time later he discovered a substantial entry for her grandson, Dr John Dougall, in *Who's Who in Glasgow in 1909*. There was, of course, plenty of interesting information about John Dougall himself, including a photograph. However, the entry mentioned his relative 'Sir' Duncan McArthur, repeating the story that he had been aboard HMS *Victory* at Trafalgar. Finally, a copy of an article about Duncan was discovered in Glasgow City Archives, showing that he had in fact served on board the *Victory*, but about ten years before the Battle of Trafalgar. Also, although not actually knighted, he was awarded the CB, one rank below that of knighthood. This Duncan was a brother of Florence and son of Duncan, a gardener in Glasgow.

Amongst the traditions in your family folklore there may be claims to a relationship to a historical figure or to the nobility which you will be keen to investigate further. We will return to descents from the nobility later on in the book.

TALES OF THE UNEXPECTED

In the course of your researches, you may uncover a totally unexpected relationship. This happened in the course of one of our own pieces of research, when, having located a great-great-grandmother's death certificate, her mother's maiden name was found to be Munnings. As an interesting example of the unreliability of some sources, the mother's Christian name was recorded as Elizabeth, whereas when the great-great-grandmother's baptism was traced, her mother turned out to be Sarah Green Munnings. Sarah was a sister of William Green Munnings, the grandfather of Sir Alfred Munnings, a famous painter, best known for his paintings of horses and as a controversial President of the Royal Academy.

PRIVATE DETECTIVE WORK

Family history research involves a considerable amount of detective work, often described as being like piecing together a jigsaw. This aspect can prove quite exciting. As family lines lead off in different directions you could find yourself researching the history of an area, an occupation or an industry with which your family was connected and as a result gaining new historical knowledge and insights. History can be given an added relevance when you know of your family's involvement. It becomes more personalised and has an added interest.

PRACTICAL BENEFITS

Those of you with a more practical motive behind your interest may have found that for legal or religious reasons you are required to undertake some research into your family's past. Anyone claiming a hereditary title in the United Kingdom must provide genealogical proof to substantiate their claim. In some European countries, proof of nobility over a certain period of time ensured the right to tax exemptions and entry to the army or civil service at a minimum rank and in some societies it has been necessary to show a family's high status to qualify for office. Although such requirements may appear to apply mainly to the upper classes, the average individual may also encounter similar needs. If an individual dies without leaving a will and has no known relatives, members of the family would be required to prove their relationship if they wished to inherit anything. Again, in medieval England, unfree tenants could not bring a case to court since they had no legal standing, but if they could prove a relationship to freemen, the case could go ahead. As a result, English medieval records contain genealogies of ordinary people recorded for this purpose.

Members of the Church of Jesus Christ of Latter-day Saints, or Mormons as they are usually known, have a religious motive behind their enthusiasm for genealogy. Mormons are required to trace as many as possible of their ancestors so that they can be baptised by proxy. They believe that only those baptised by a Mormon priest can achieve full salvation and that this can be done for dead relatives whom they believe would have become Mormons if they had had the opportunity. As a result, the Mormon Church has undertaken a vast amount of work in microfilming and inputting genealogical data to computer files. This has been of great benefit to genealogists throughout the world and as you might expect the Mormons now have an enormous storehouse of information, contained in a huge underground library near Salt Lake City, USA. Some of the direct benefits of the work of the Mormons to other researchers such as ourselves will be mentioned later in the book.

FAMILY MEDICAL HISTORY

It has been known for long enough that some diseases and medical conditions can be inherited and, probably encouraged by the tremendous advances over the last few years in tracking down the genetic origins of various diseases, there has been an increasing interest in the tracing and recording of family medical history. The value of this is becoming more evident as the prospect of new treatments and even cures becomes a real possibility. Perhaps by researching the diseases of past members of your family you may be able to discover the likely health problems of present and future generations, making it much easier to identify any appropriate new treatments which could even in some cases save lives. One of the recent books on this topic is actually subtitled 'How tracing your family medical history can save your life'. Family medical history can be recorded in what are known as genograms. These are a specific form of family tree which use standard symbols to display family relationships and are particularly suited for recording the medical history of families. Due to the difficulty in gathering accurate diagnoses of causes of death beyond a few generations, genograms usually cover about three to four generations at best. Computer software is available to draw genograms as well as the more traditional type of family tree. More on this subject, including the basics of drawing genograms with the standard symbols and software you can use, can be found on Cyndi's List (www.CyndisList.com).

Because of the prospect of future treatments and cures, there is a move to 'bank' DNA samples which may at some point alert individuals to genetic diseases in their family. DNA is the genetic material which provides the blueprint for each individual's characteristics. DNA banking has been taking place for some years in the fields of criminal investigation in the United Kingdom and the United States and also in the US Department of Defense where all new service personnel enlisted since 1994 have had their DNA banked. For the reasons given, it is likely to become more common for private individuals to take this opportunity.

GENETICS

This leads us on to the study of genetics itself, the advances in which are the cause of the increasing importance of 'medical genealogy'. Talk of genetics and DNA is never absent for long from the news these days. This usually concerns the identification of specific genes responsible for diseases or other characteristics but sometimes relates to theories about the origins of man. Some work had been done previously on diseases such as haemophilia and porphyria, but now much more common diseases are being looked at, like cystic fibrosis, Huntington's chorea, Alzheimer's disease and Rett syndrome. These developments could have a considerable effect on our lives.

The basis of the great strides made in this area of scientific research is a massive long-term project named the Human Genome Project, in which scientists in various parts of the world have been mapping the human genome, the complete set of genes contained in human DNA. It is an enormous task, but a draft has now been made and it is hoped that a detailed map will be completed in 2003. This will locate the position of all the various genes, including disease genes.

Two of the smaller countries of the world are leading the way in planning large-scale research on genetic diseases, with one already in operation. DeCODE Genetics, a company based in Iceland, has been given permission by the government to create an Icelandic Health Sector Database, to be operated for twelve years. The Database is now in existence and uses DNA samples from the population of about 275,000. This is a controversial development, since the information is automatically included in the Database unless individuals specifically object. If employers and insurance companies could gain access to this information, genetic discrimination might result, but of course DeCODE assures critics that security measures will be stringent. Because there has been very little immigration into Iceland for the last 1,100 years, the small population has many genetic similarities and most are descended from the original settlers. Iceland has excellent health records and genealogical records, which is a great help in identifying disease genes. Using genealogical data, the company can identify large extended families, sometimes linked over more than ten generations and including individuals with particular diseases. This Book of Icelanders has been made available to the Icelandic people and it is hoped to put it on the Web. DNA samples from closely and distantly related sufferers from specific diseases are compared and this helps to identify disease genes. So far, twelve diseases with possible genetic causes have been identified and in a number of these the region of the disease gene has been located.

In Estonia, another project is at the planning stage. The Estonian Genome Foundation, again with government backing, hopes to store genetic data from at least two-thirds of the Estonian population of 1.4 million people. This differs from the Icelandic project in that the Estonians would take part on a voluntary basis. The aims of the project are to improve the understanding of the genetic code in general and to pinpoint disease genes, leading to the development of drugs to target inherited diseases.

As well as the relationships between genealogy, genetics and health, there are also applications of genetics in the more traditional areas of genealogy. We should always remember that all of our ancestors are important in creating us as individuals. As well as passing on susceptibilities to particular diseases, they also pass on many characteristics and talents, such as colour of hair, colour of eyes or musical talent, as seen in the Bach family, which included a large number of prominent musicians and composers. With the DNA testing which is now available, we can establish certain things about descents and relationships. Two important examples of this can be illustrated, firstly in connection with the family of Tsar Nicholas II of Russia and secondly in the case of 'Cheddar Man'. The Tsar and his family were murdered during the Russian Revolution and it is now possible to confirm that the remains thought to be those of his family are genuine and also that Anna Anderson, who claimed to be Princess Anastasia, one of the Tsar's daughters, was not related to him. The other case is that of 'Cheddar Man' in England. His remains were found in a Stone Age burial from about 7000 BC. DNA samples were taken and individuals living in the area were tested and as a result it was found that a local school teacher named Adrian Targett was related to Cheddar Man through his mother's ancestry. This was proved by testing mitochondrial DNA.

There are at present two methods which can be used to prove relationships. One tests the Y chromosome, which is passed on through the male line only. There is little or no change in the Y chromosome over a long period of time and each Y chromosome posseses a haplotype which should match for individuals related through the male line. The other method uses analysis of mitochondrial DNA, which is passed from a female to her children and so this method can trace relationships through the maternal line.

It is now possible to have these tests done at a cost, or to obtain a sampling kit for possible DNA banking. A company called Oxford Ancestors has been set up recently to do this type of work for genealogists and offers services using both methods of testing relationships: using Y chromosomes and mitochondrial DNA. The cost is still high for the average family historian, but services of this sort will probably be more frequently used in the future.

Author Graham Holton has been involved with research undertaken by researchers at University College London, making use of the Y chromosome. Samples were taken with a swab from the inside of the cheek and then analysed to produce a haplotype. Descendants in the male line from a common male ancestor should have the same or very similar haplotype, but there are various reasons why this may result in no match when one was expected, as happened in this case. There were, however, 12 matches on the database of 762, with individuals of different surnames, who must be related in the male line but with a common ancestor dating back to before the establishment of fixed surnames. Perhaps long before that time.

Mitochondrial DNA is inherited through the female line by both males and females, but is not passed on any further by males. Testing for this material can prove descents through the female line from a common female ancestor.

For more information, check the Bibliography and Web sites such as Oxford Ancestors.

IMPORTANCE OF FAMILY HISTORY TO OTHER SUBJECTS

We would like to point out here that although family history is of obvious interest for the reasons already mentioned, its importance extends much further, into the fields of local, economic and social history and historical demography. If we take a magnifying glass to the whole expanse of history we see the local history of each area and then, with a stronger lens, the family history of those who make up each individual community. In focusing on the individuals within a community, family history can illuminate and bring new perspectives to a study of a particular locality. Whether of high or low status, the family about which we are gathering information played a role in local society which was probably similar to that played by other families of comparable status. You may have information on the type of life lived by a whole section of the community or perhaps facts about a particular occupation important in the area. These are the sort of details which a local historian will need in order to provide a representative picture of life in the locality concerned. Such information can also be drawn upon by economic and social historians working on a broader scale and in particular by those studying historical demography.

Notable in this field in England has been the Cambridge Group for the History of Population and Social Structure, in particular Peter Laslett, R. S. Schofield and E. A. Wrigley. Since the 1960s they have been studying records of specific English parishes and applying statistical methods in order to analyse the populations and thereby draw conclusions. They have studied literacy, by looking at the ability to sign marriage registers or other documents, and social structure from census returns and other listings of inhabitants. The main procedures they have used, however, are aggregation and family reconstitution. Aggregation uses the total figures of baptisms, marriages and burials from parish registers and is a fairly quick means of analysing population trends. The types of information gained are: the growth or decline of population; baptism, marriage and burial rates; marital fertility rates; infant mortality rates; mobility of population; and illegitimacy rates. Family reconstitution, although a much slower method, allows a more detailed and accurate analysis.

In this case, information is gathered from various sources about members of particular families in order to 'reconstitute' them. Calculations are then made to establish: age at marriage; age at burial; age at the end of marriage; length of marriage; age of mother at baptisms of children; interval between baptisms; and number of children. This information tells us a lot about the sociology of the family at different times and in different places and used together with data on the weather and harvest yields, the impact of epidemics and so on, can greatly increase our knowledge of the social and economic history of England.

In the process of family reconstitution, the historical demographers are doing much the same as the family historian but for a large number of families in a parish. The conclusions which they draw can provide a context within which to place our own family. Was our family and its individual members unusual in the time and place in question or did they follow the normal pattern of family life? These are the sort of questions that we would like to answer and the methods and work of historical demographers may help us to do that.

Apart from the work of D. F. Macdonald, *Scotland's Shifting Population, 1770–1850*, published in 1937, the population history of Scotland received little attention until the 1970s, which saw the publication of *Scottish Population History from the 17th Century to the 1930s*, edited by Michael Flinn (1977). Over the last few years there have been various research projects on the subject based at the Universities of Strathclyde, Aberdeen, Glasgow and Lancaster and conclusions based on this research have appeared in various publications.

One particularly useful new tool now available for the study of historical demography is the 1881 British Census on CD-ROM. As we will show later in the book, it is possible to search for names throughout Scotland, England and Wales. Searches on occupations, addresses, ages and places of birth can also be made on individual regions, the last of these allowing the study of population movements.

GENEALOGY IN THE PAST

Throughout the ages, genealogy has varied in importance, depending on place and period and for widely differing reasons. Genealogists in the ancient world often traced the origins of a family or race back to gods and heroes. Genealogy helped to provide an extra unity to societies which emphasised kinship and demonstrated the necessary status which could entitle a family to an office, title or ownership of land. For example, Julius Caesar claimed descent from the goddess Venus, through the Trojan Aeneas, while the Greeks Hippocrates and Aristotle both believed they were descended from Asclepius, the god of medicine. The Bible contains many genealogies tracing descents from Adam and Eve and in both China and Japan in ancient times, family records were well maintained. Most Chinese families kept a Generation Book, usually updated about every thirty years, which recorded births, marriages and deaths along with other information about the families. The Japanese government set up an office in 761 to record clan genealogies and within a hundred years or so more than 1,100 clans had been registered.

Medieval times saw the production of Norse sagas, Bede's *Ecclesiastical History of the English People,* the *Anglo-Saxon Chronicle* and Geoffrey of Monmouth's *History of the Kings of Britain,* in all of which a great interest in genealogy is evident. Descents from gods and heroes are numerous, but in most cases quite fictitious. In Scotland, the sennachies of the Highland clans were the bards who maintained the genealogical traditions of the clans. Their function was of great importance, not just because they could relate the ancestry of the members of the clan, linking them together and in some cases with the clan chief, but also because this information determined the rights of families to hold land and has been compared to the title deed in the feudal system.

From the sixteenth century, many genealogies were drawn up to prove the right to a coat of arms and to provide merchant and professional families with a high social status which they saw as important. By the end of the nineteenth century the production of genealogies was becoming much more scientific and the fabulous concoctions of the medieval genealogists were rejected. This reaction perhaps tended to go too far and the study of genealogy had reached a reasonably balanced approach by the late twentieth century. However, particularly with the advent of the Internet, a tendency towards assuming links based solely on secondary sources is beginning to creep in.

FACTORS IN TRACING ANCESTRY

Sir Anthony Wagner, in his book *English Genealogy,* identified four factors governing the tracing of ancestry: status, record, name and continuity.

The status of a family in general affects the extent to which it appears in the records. The status may be that of a noble family, of land owners, of holders of public office or of a merchant family. As we shall see, as a result of social mobility, there could be a considerable movement in and out of such families and so you may find that your own family is at some periods much more easily traceable than at others.

The existence of records is obviously of vital importance in successfully tracing your family history. From time to time records may have been lost, damaged, destroyed or have been kept negligently. Some parish registers begin in the sixteenth century, others not until the eighteenth, which poses considerable problems for the genealogist.

Names, both Christian names and surnames, can range from the very common to the very unusual and an unusual name or combination of names can make a tremendous difference to your ability to identify the individual you are seeking. In city parishes with large numbers of baptisms, marriages and burials, there may be a number of persons of the same name registered round about the same date, given that the name is a fairly common one. On the other hand, if you are searching for an unusual name, there is a much greater chance of a correct identification. Customs for choosing Christian names, particularly in Scotland, can also lend a helping hand to the researcher. This is discussed in Chapter 9.

The last of Wagner's factors is that of continuity. A family which has a continuous connection with one place is normally much easier to trace than one which moved about a lot. Movement from place to place often poses problems in family history research. It could take place on a small scale from parish to parish and was often more common than might be imagined. Movement within a ten-mile radius was very common in the past, but a move of a greater distance can be difficult for the family historian to trace. The greatest migration which affected the population as a whole was the movement from the country to the towns during the Industrial Revolution, particularly in the first half of the nineteenth century. Scotland also saw a great influx of Irish immigrants in the nineteenth century with the largest numbers settling in the Glasgow area but with significant numbers also in Edinburgh and Dundee. There have been other groups of immigrants in the past, but on a very much smaller scale. Continuity can also be evident in a long connection with a particular piece of land, an occupation or an institution. All such connections tend to improve the chance of successful research.

You are unlikely to be blessed with a combination of all these factors and although your family may have been resident in one place for several centuries, you may have the misfortune to discover that the records are poor and only began relatively recently. Perhaps one of the other factors may provide extra assistance.

You may now be asking what are the likely chances of success. Although you may hear of people who claim to be descended from Normans who came over with William the Conqueror, this is extremely unlikely. It seems that no one can prove a continuous descent in the male line from a companion of William at Hastings. There are a handful of very long descents in the male line which have been proved, a good example being the family of Arden, which is descended from Aelfwine, Sheriff of Warwickshire before 1066. In Scotland, the various branches of the family of Dundas can trace their ancestry back to Helias de Dundas, living in the early twelfth century. These descents are exceptional and probably on average you would be fortunate to trace back to the seventeenth century. You should certainly have a good chance of reaching the mid-eighteenth century.

SOCIAL MOBILITY

We have already mentioned in passing the question of noble descents and social mobility in relation to a family's status. Social mobility in Britain was quite marked in contrast to other parts of Europe. It can involve a decline in status from one extreme to the other or may show movement up and down over the centuries. Some examples can illustrate this point well.

Having researched the late Queen Mother's sixty-four ancestors in the seventh generation back, genealogists discovered that they included two dukes, three earls, a viscount, a baron, a duke's daughter, a marquess's daughter, an earl's daughter, a bishop's daughter, six country gentlemen, a director of the East India Company, a banker, three clergymen, the daughter of a Huguenot refugee, the landlord of the George Inn, Stamford, a London toyman and a London plumber. This research applied to ancestry, but examples can also be found in descents that have been researched. A peerage claim for the barony of Dudley, which was in abeyance from 1757 to 1914, brought to light the fact that the co-heirs, who were all descendants of King Henry VII (d. 1509), consisted of a butcher, a gamekeeper, a toll gate keeper, a baker's wife and a tailor's wife.

One of the authors' ancestry provides an interesting example of social mobility. The author's branch of the Holton family moved to Scotland in the 1880s when his great-grandfather, then working as a commercial traveller, settled in Glasgow. He began his working life as a hosiery warehouseman and came from a family of farmers and butchers in Suffolk. His maternal grandfather, Anthony Hicks, had also been a farmer, but Anthony's mother, Sarah Timperley, although her immediate ancestors were Suffolk farmers, was the third generation in descent from Thomas Timperley, Lord of the Manor of Hintlesham. This family was for several generations closely associated with the Mowbray and Howard Dukes of Norfolk and William Timperley actually married Margaret Howard, an illegitimate daughter of Thomas Howard, 3rd Duke of Norfolk, in the early sixteenth century. The 3rd Duke, who was a major figure in the Court of Henry VIII, was descended, through the Mowbrays, from Thomas of Brotherton, the second son of King Edward I. If you do happen to prove a connection with a royal family, quite amazing ancestors can be traced. For example, Edward I was descended from William the Conqueror, St Margaret of Scotland and the Emperor Charlemagne, while his second wife, Margaret of France, the mother of Thomas of Brotherton, numbered the Byzantine Emperor Constantine VII and Charlemagne amongst her ancestors.

We hope that this chapter has given you some background firstly on the history and uses of genealogy and the importance of family history to other historical studies and secondly on various factors which will affect the course of your own researches.

CHAPTER 1

GATHERING INFORMATION FROM YOUR FAMILY

If you are setting out on the trail of tracing your ancestors and collecting the history of your family together, the first step should really be to try to gather as much information as possible that you already know, or that other family members know. You may find that information readily, or you may find that it is tucked away in the recesses of someone's mind, or in the depths of some relative's cupboard or attic.

It would be possible to work back, just simply knowing your own name and your date of birth, but this would be a very clinical way of working. You could miss out on the really interesting flesh to be put on the bones of genealogy, the warmth and humour of family life, the anecdotes about the characteristics of members of previous generations.

The first source of information should be yourself and family members.

This is an extremely important first step – to try to gather and collate all information from the living relatives to whom you can gain access.

You may be surprised at how much genealogical information is stored in families, once you start to probe a bit further. You may know a surprising amount yourself, when you start to formalise or organise that information. Other family members may have access to invaluable records, certificates, photographs, family recollections, rumours and scandals.

WHEN SHOULD YOU START?

There is really no time like the present. You should be prepared especially to take any suitable opportunity to talk to members of the older generations within your family about their brothers and sisters, parents, aunts, uncles and cousins and take careful note of what they have to tell you. If you postpone the start of this process, then members of the older generation may well have departed, taking all the gems of personal detail about your ancestors with them, never to be recovered.

Of course, you will have to approach the matter with a great deal of tact – if you suddenly ask a relative that you haven't bothered with for the last twenty years to give you all the most intimate details about the family, to hand over certificates and photographs at the first meeting, you are unlikely to achieve anything apart from instant suspicion of your motives, and a permanent refusal to have any further dealings with you! You must try to establish a relationship of mutual trust, genuine interest and concern. This will take time and effort, but can pay huge dividends in the longer run.

WHAT KIND OF MATERIAL ARE YOU LOOKING FOR?

Names
Dates
Places
Occupations

These may take the more official form of birth certificates, marriage certificates, death certificates. However, other less formal or recollected verbal information is worth recording, but should not be accepted as absolutely accurate.

Further information, of a less cold statistical nature, is very useful as you build up a picture of your family history, to find out what made your forebears tick, to trace shared characteristics through the generations and so on.

Some headings (though this is not an exhaustive list) could be:

Appearance
Characteristics
Habits
Motives
Odd Sayings
Family Legend(s)
Old Photographs
Memorial Cards

Indentures
Granny's Birthday Book
School Reports
Army Rolls of Honour
Family Bible

HOW SHOULD I APPROACH THE GAINING OF INFORMATION FROM RELATIVES?

As stated previously, this has to be done carefully, sympathetically and tactfully. Be careful not to over-tire anyone. Talk about people in the way the relative will know them. Don't press for specific dates, but try to relate to world, national, local or personal events, for example 'The War', or 'when you were at school', or 'before your brother left home'. An unobtrusive tape-recording could be taken, checking first that the interviewee would be comfortable with this, rather than scribbling notes and having to ask for repetition of some detail.

SOME KEYNOTES OF SUCCESS

Don't be in a hurry to go somewhere else, or over-stay your welcome. Try to make them relax; you want them to feel that you are genuinely interested in the other people and themselves. Make a point of recording as much information as possible, including those details that may not seem important at the time but might turn out to be very helpful later.

A GOOD STRATEGY

Don't go to visit a relative with a view to gaining all the information you can without offering anything in return – this will immediately arouse suspicion. You should try to add some information to which you have access, even if that is simply the latest news and pictures of your branch of the current generation.
Some possible items to take with you could be:

Family photographs
Mystery pictures
A small tape-recorder
An incomplete or outline family tree (leaving room for discussion on details)

A SYSTEM FOR RECORDING THIS INFORMATION

You may or may not decide that a small tape-recorder would be suitable for recording information gained during your visit with an elderly relative. No matter what you decide, it is vital that you record in some permanent, readable form all the information that you have already, or have gained during this interview. An example of a family questionnaire form which should cover all the potential areas of interest is given in Appendix 5.

This could be posted to a relative, or could simply be used as a structure to record the results of your meeting. It is important to say at this point that although the bare facts of names, places and dates are very important to build up the structure or skeleton of your family history, the anecdotes about relatives are much more enlivening. It can be quite exciting to hear of the eccentricities, pet likes and dislikes, or sense of humour of someone who previously had just been a name on a yellowing certificate or the subject of a rather staid sepia photograph.

Information about the existence of other sources of family knowledge, such as a family Bible, or news of a distant cousin also interested in the family can open up new vistas of possibilities.

At this stage you shouldn't worry that there are more blanks than completed spaces. It is very likely that the information which you already have or have been given isn't 100 per cent accurate.

Later on, in Chapter 3, we will show you that there are ways to use your possibly inaccurate information to lead you to reliable sources of accurate dates and so on.

Another possible means of recording information is an individual record of significant details about one particular relative or ancestor. Depending upon your preference, you may find this easier to handle during an interview. It has the limitation that it does not allow for extra, exciting anecdotes to be added, but caters solely for the bare statistical bones of the individual concerned. Here are some broad headings which could be used:

First Names
Surname
When Born
Where Born
When Baptised
Where Baptised
Father's Name

Father's Occupation
Mother's Name
Parents' Date of Marriage
Parents' Place of Marriage
Date of Marriage
Date of Death
Place of Death
Cause of Death

Whatever method you decide to use for keeping your records, it is very important to be methodical and well organised. So many of us involved in family history research have, in our enthusiasm, jotted down notes on different subjects and from different sources all in the same notebook. This soon makes it very much more difficult to locate information than it need be, and it takes a great deal of work to reorganise the data at a later stage. With some careful planning at the outset, this situation can be avoided.

MEANS OF DISPLAYING A FAMILY TREE

THE DROP LINE CHART

You will probably already have seen the most common form of graphically displaying a family tree – in the form of a 'tree' with the twigs and branches decked out with leaves, each leaf representing a family member.

The links back to the common ancestor are shown moving back through the twigs to the larger branches and finally to the trunk. This kind of tree can most commonly be seen in museums, representing the genealogy of aristocratic or royal families.

However, a simpler form of this can be seen in figure 1.1.

The oldest generation is shown at the top of the chart, with succeeding generations branching out lower down, with links moving downwards normally through marriage, which is indicated by an 'equals' (=) sign. The same generations can be seen side by side along the same row on the chart. Sometimes if there are many generations and large families, this can demand very wide paper or extremely small, cramped writing. It may be impossible to arrange for all those of the same generation to appear on the same row. The details you include could vary widely from the basic names with dates of birth or baptism, and death or burial, to more elaborate entries with places of birth, marriage and death, date of marriage, occupations and so on.

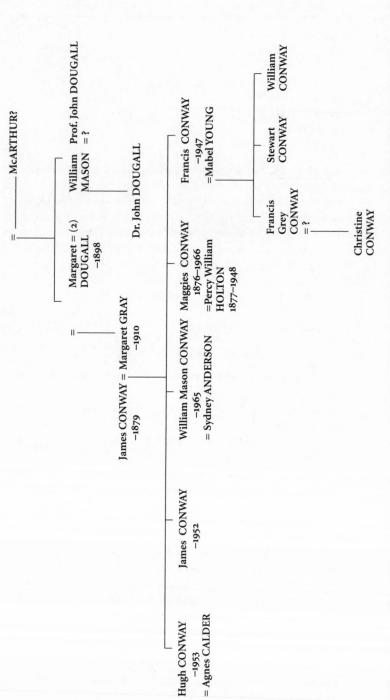

Figure 1.1 Example of a drop line chart.

Figure 1.2 Example of a birth brief.

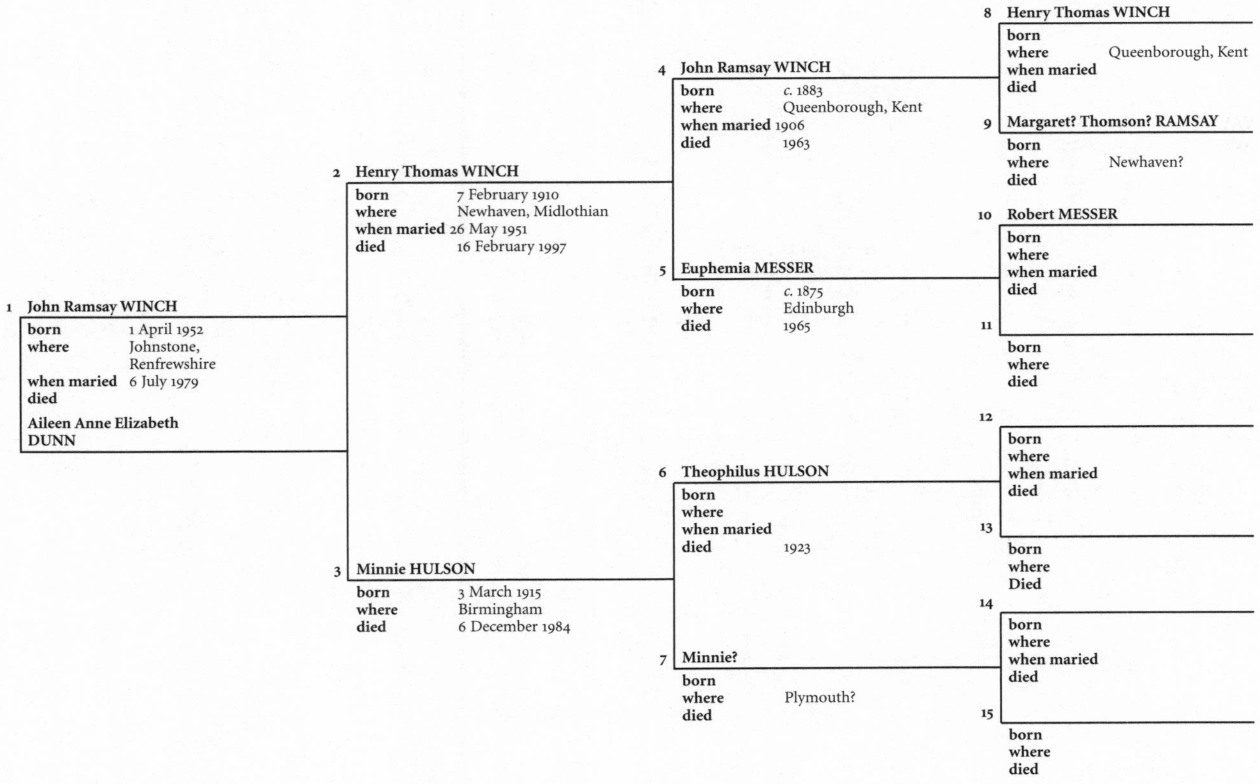

THE BIRTH BRIEF

As you can see in figure 1.2, the birth brief begins on the left-hand side of the page, with one individual.

As you proceed to the right, you move back in time to the parents, grandparents, great-grandparents and so on, with each generation of ancestors arranged in columns. It is possible to have a number of these birth briefs, each beginning with a different individual, to record various lines of ancestors. The limitation is, of course, that it does not accommodate brothers, sisters and their descendants, as the drop line chart does.

THE CIRCULAR TREE

Like the birth brief, this can be a useful starting tool for building up the framework of a family tree. It is limited in that it does not show brothers and sisters, but only parents of one child. You can think of it as a cross-section of a tree trunk, with succeeding rings radiating outwards.

Normally, you would start out with yourself in the central 'core' of the circle or 'trunk' and move outwards to your mother and father in the next 'shell', then their parents in the succeeding shell, and so on. A number of these charts can be used, with different interesting individuals forming the central core.

This will suffice as a starting place to record your information. As your research starts to build up, we will see that increasingly there are commonly available information technology tools which will help you to keep track of the vast quantities of interesting detail which you will accumulate surprisingly quickly, without resorting to pencil and rubber, screwing up paper and rewriting vast tracts of information.

Figure 1.3 Example of a circular tree.

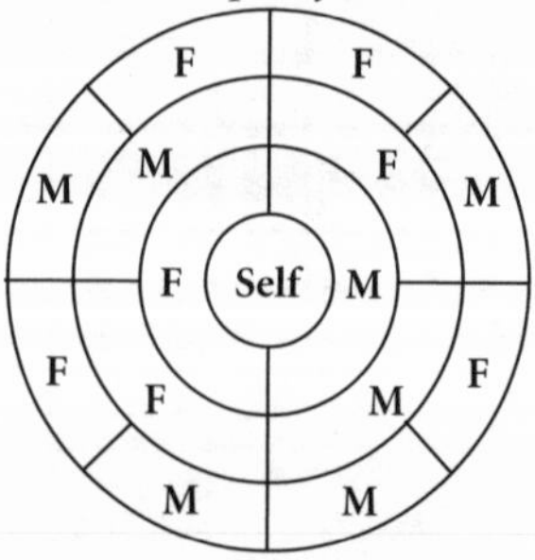

Figure 1.4 A completed family information form.

Family Information Form

Please give full names & previous surname(s)

Your Name John Ramsay Winch | | **Husband / Wife** Aileen A. E. Dunn
(& maiden name)

Date & Place of Birth / Baptism — 1 April 1952, Johnstone | | 22 April 1953, Lennoxtown
Date & Place of Marriage — 6 July 1979, Lennoxtown
Date & Place of Death / Burial
Occupation — University Lecturer | | Primary School Teacher

Your Children

	Douglas John	Kirsten Anne	Louise Amy

Date & Place of Birth / Baptism — Douglas John: 2 April 1983, Paisley | Kirsten Anne: 19 February 1986, Paisley | Louise Amy: 13 January 1991, Paisley
Date & Place of Marriage
Name of Husband / Wife
Date & Place of Death / Burial
Occupation

Their Children

1
2
3

Your Father | | **Your Mother** (& maiden name)
Name — Henry Thomas Winch | | Minnie Ethel Theodora Hulson
Date & Place of Birth / Baptism — 7 February 1910, Leith | | 3 March 1915, Birmingham
Date & Place of Marriage — 26 May 1951, Birmingham | | 6 December 1994, Renfrew
Date & Place of Death / Burial — 16 February 1997, Renfrew | | Primary School Teacher
Occupation — Draughtsman

Your FATHER's Father | | **His Wife** (& maiden name)
Name — John Ramsay Winch | | Euphemia G? R? Messer
Date & Place of Birth / Baptism — 1880s, England? | | 1875, Edinburgh
Date & Place of Marriage — 26 June 1906, where? | | 1965, Paisley
Date & Place of Death / Burial — 1963, Paisley
Occupation — 03M, Royal Engineers

Your MOTHER's Father

Name   Theophilus Hulson
Date & Place of Birth / Baptism   ?
Date & Place of Marriage   ?
Date & Place of Death / Burial   1924, ?
Occupation   Admiralty Overseer

His Wife (& maiden name)
Minnie ?
?
?
Weston-Super-Mare

Other Family Members

Do you know any other information about other relatives, such as uncles, aunts, great-uncles, great-aunts, cousins, etc.?

1. Full name   Relationship
   Details

2. Full name   Relationship
   Details

3. Full name   Relationship
   Details

Family Traditions

Are there any family traditions / stories which you can recall?
My great-grandfather, called Henry Thomas Winch, lived in Queenborough, Kent and sailed a Thames Barge.

Do you know of the existence of a Family Bible? Does it have family details? Where is it?
There is a page torn out of my father's mother's old family Bible with some obscure birth and death dates.

CASE STUDY

Figure 1.4 shows how a completed family 'questionnaire' or 'information' form might look at the early stages of your research. Indeed, this represents the quantity of information which one of the authors had at his disposal at the start of his family history investigations.

You will have taken some time, firstly to investigate all of this information by means of family sources and then to document what you have discovered. It would be a pity, therefore, if both old documentary evidence (such as certificates, old photographs and so on) and any new documentation which you have created (such as a draft family tree) were to be at risk of unnecessary deterioration. In Chapter 2 we go on to consider how best to ensure that such materials are preserved.

RECORDING AND STORING INFORMATION

Once you have carried out some research into your family history at home, from relatives, and at a later stage in New Register House and local libraries, you will very soon accumulate quite a considerable quantity of detailed information. Unless you have a systematic way of storing that information, it can very easily become confused and you can misunderstand the links and relationships. It's amazing how quickly important details can be lost or mislaid, especially if you rely on memory alone.

In this chapter we hope to illustrate the pros and cons of some methods of storing the harvest of your research, in order that you can keep it secure, yet gain ready access to update your family tree in the light of your latest research results.

As a general rule, you should always clearly distinguish between the information you have found in the original sources and the information you have built up based on these sources. The source material should be stored quite separately from your conclusions.

Indeed, you may require to return to your original source material as your own research (or that of future generations) progresses in order to correct or update previous conclusions. Therefore it is most important that this valuable source material is stored in a manner which will help to preserve it.

PAPER RECORDS

You can, of course, simply write the information down on paper. This is, naturally, an improvement on memory supplemented by notes on scraps of paper. The difficulty which can arise with this is that with further investigation, details will need to be changed, expanded and deleted. An improvement might be to store information on individuals by means of a sorted card-index system. This would allow for new individuals to be inserted in chronological or alphabetical order, and for additional notes to be added to individual cards.

We have produced some sample sheets which could be used as the basis of a paper records system which you might like to use. There are separate sheets for a variety of purposes, and use of these will encourage you to note the information down in a systematic fashion. Examples of these can be seen in Appendix 5.

KEEPING TRACK BY COMPUTER

The greatest and most significant advantage of using a computer system to assist in the maintenance of your family history research is that many different types of information – narrative, dates, relationships, illustrations, family trees and so on – can be stored in the one compact space, namely on one computer system with perhaps a number of additional disks.

There are some aspects of your family tree that can never be stored on a computer system. Naturally, original certificates, photographs and papers still need to be stored, preferably in a secure and fireproof cabinet. Though the making of copies can never supplant the thrill of finding and retaining original documents, it is, however, possible to scan copies of the original photographs and documents and store them as graphics files on disk.

In the very gradual process of building up the picture of your family history, the possibility of storing incomplete information which can be added to in a piecemeal fashion, without the need for a complete rewrite of the information, is one of the main strengths of computer use for this purpose. There is the additional benefit that paper copies of the information can be printed out whenever you require, without having to arrange for photocopying or storing large quantities of duplicated paper.

WORD PROCESSING

A normal word processing system of any variety with which you are familiar is of enormous value to you in the pursuit of building up the narrative of your family history. You can write a partially complete narrative and return to it with amendments and additions at any time as your investigations proceed. In the case of the word processing software produced in the last five years or so, it is possible to include pictures (or graphics) which can help to enliven your narrative, and to save the illustrated narrative as a word-processed file on disk. If you have old photographs, rather than stick them on to your page, it is possible to use a scanner attached to the computer which will copy them in a suitable form for storage along with your text as part of your word-processed file. It is also possible to enhance the scanned image if the original is somewhat faded. This then allows you to keep the precious original photographs safely filed away for posterity.

USING DATABASES

If, for example, you have lists of census details which may be connected with your family, it will be of value to put them into a database. The fields of the database should follow the different columns in the census enumeration sheet, such as name, relationship to head of household, age, marital status and occupation. Your collection can then be browsed through, searched, put into different orders and printed out in the order you wish. Another effective use of a database would be to store information which you have gathered from the International Genealogical Index (IGI).

USING SPREADSHEETS

If you simply have a set of information which is best stored in the form of a table, you may find it simpler to use a spreadsheet such as Microsoft Excel. See figure 2.2 on page 42 for an example of one use of a spreadsheet.

SPECIALIST GENEALOGICAL SOFTWARE

Some basic requirements for choosing suitable specialist software for storing your family history information are as follows. The program should allow you to record all data that you discover during your research, including conflicting data for the same event, and you should be able to document where each piece of information that you record was obtained.

Here are some key features to look for in family history software:

Integrity The program should not create new data by itself. If the program adds data such as a 'married name' the user should have control over the process.

Recording names Adequate space and fields should be available for recording names and there should be a means to record all name variants a person might use in his/her life.

Recording dates All standard forms of date entries should be accepted and the user should be able to choose the form in which dates are displayed in the program. The program should allow a 'sort date' or other means to control the sorting of data in the program views and reports.

Recording places A facility should be available to record place names.

Recording roles Many events in your database will have more than one participant. Some programs now have tools to link all of those persons to that event and to allow each differing role to be output to narrative reports.

Multiple parents The software should allow linking a child to not only their natural parents but also to adopted parents and handling other non-traditional relationships.

Multiple spouses The software should also allow linking a person to more than one spouse.

Multimedia There should be provisions for linking multimedia objects (photos, sound, video) to individuals and events and to be able to incorporate those images into reports.

Source documentation It will be advantageous to record the source of any information that you enter into your database to provide substantiation for your research and to tell other researchers where they can locate the data that you are reporting. Programs should include the ability to record citation detail which links the event to the source and records the repository where the source was obtained.

Evidence evaluation A provision should exist to enter a 'surety' value so that you can record your judgment about the validity of any data that you enter.

Searching and sorting The software should provide tools to find individuals and to designate subsets of your data for export and for printing.

Research log Your program should give you the ability to record tasks as you discover what needs to be done and to print a useful report to aid your next trip to a repository.

Data import Some programs permit direct import from the databases produced by other software packages and every major genealogy program supports GEDCOM version 5.5 (GEnealogical Data COMmunication), a standard developed to facilitate exchanging computerised genealogical data.

Data export GEDCOM data transfer is limited to only certain data that fits the specification. Since the more sophisticated programs can record data for which no explicit provision is made in the GEDCOM standard, there may be limits to how much of the data recorded in one piece of software can be transferred to another via GEDCOM. At present, there is no alternative to the GEDCOM system for genealogical information exchange.

Report output To aid your research, you may need to be able to produce lists of subsets of people or events as defined by a 'filter'. When you contact a new relative, you may like to be able to provide him/her with a concise and readable report such as a pedigree or compact descendant chart to show the stage of your research. At the other end of the spectrum, databases can help in the production of reports such as the family history you have been planning to write. You should, for example, be able to create a readable narrative report with a table of contents, footnotes or endnotes to annotate your data, a bibliography, and one or more indexes. Your report should be exported in a format acceptable to the word processor of your choice for final editing. If you include graphical images, the report should include links to the external image files inserted into the proper places in the text.

Web page creation The facility to convert your data to Web page (HTML) format and some aids for Web page creation are becoming more valuable with the increasing use of the Internet by genealogists.

Backup Your program should have backup capabilities to safeguard your data.

SOFTWARE FOR PC AND WINDOWS

Personal Ancestral File (PAF)

PAF is a 32-bit application that runs under the Windows operating system. PAF can be downloaded for free at www.familysearch.org.

PAF's Edit Individual screen has sections for Personal (name elements, sex), Events (birth, christening, death, burial), LDS Ordinances (displayed optionally), Other Events (predefined or custom) and Other (name variants, cause of death, physical description and custom ID). A simple marriage record screen records the marriage and has a divorce flag. Other data may go in the individual or marriage note fields. Data in the note fields may be 'regular' (text) or 'tagged' (text denoted by named tags). A leading character may mark notes as printable or confidential.

Name and place fields are limited to 120 characters. The Edit Individual screen allows for married name, 'also known as' and nickname. Additional names can be entered in the Other Events section.

Children can be linked to multiple sets of parents and each relationship can be marked as one of five predefined types (biological, adopted, guardian, challenged or disproved). However, you can select only one type of parent link for each set of parents and you can have only one type of parent link for any given parent.

Multimedia objects can be added to any individual or source. Default photos optionally display on the Family View screen and can be included on reports and Web pages.

One or more sources can be attached to the data and events on the Edit Individual or Marriage screen. Tagged notes can also be entered as events on the Edit Individual screen with date, place and sources. The Source screen allows full source documentation including the repository, citation details, comments, a field for recording full text and an image. A new source or repository needs to be entered only once and existing entries can be selected or edited from master lists. A source with citation details may be 'memorised' and copied to new event entries.

Advanced search tools are available, using wildcards, relationship filters and field filters. Individuals or groups can be selected for reports, GEDCOM export or editing. For example, a place spelling error can be easily corrected for all affected individuals. 'Global Search and Replace' is available.

Using 'to do' tags in the note fields allows you to build a collection of research tasks and specific subsets of these tasks may be retrieved with the search tools to generate a report for a repository visit or field trip.

The GEDCOM listing file detailing import errors can be included in the notes of each appropriate individual during the import process. This is a superb feature which greatly simplifies 'clean-up' after import.

A wide variety of reports including pedigree, custom, lists, calendar, family group, ancestry, descendants, book, individual summary and two blank forms (pedigree and family group record) can be generated. Six reports including the two book reports can be saved as Rich Text Format (RTF) files for editing in a word processor. Another Windows program, the PAF Companion, can be used with PAF for printing many of the same reports in differing formats and several additional features such as kinship report, fan chart, charts of ancestors and descendants. PAF includes tools to create Web pages. File backup/restore options are available.

Generations Family Tree

Generations is a 32-bit application that runs under the Windows operating system.

The Edit Person screen has tabs for Name (name, sex, user ID), Events (predefined or custom events with type, date, place and memo), Facts (predefined or custom facts with type and text), Notes (predefined or custom) and Flags (predefined or custom). Some items predefined as 'facts' are better suited as 'events' with dates and you can set them up as you wish. Additional name variants can be defined as events or facts. Following GEDCOM import of data, all name variants are added to the first and last name as appropriate. Basically, most data can be stored as events or facts rather than being entered into notes fields. Images can be attached to the family cards and marked as the primary image for either spouse.

If you enter a date form that Generations doesn't recognize, you will be prompted for a sort date. In addition, you can manually arrange the order of events on the event tab by dragging them.

The Edit Family screen has tabs for Marriage (date, place, memo, type and status), Children (with control of order and fifteen types of child status), Notes (predefined and custom) and Events (predefined or custom with type, date, place and memo). A child can be linked to both adoptive and biological parents (duplicate child buttons).

Sources can be entered on a source fields tab in a structured fashion or on a free form text tab. Source fields are predefined or custom and include a data field. The repository is entered in a library/archive field. A preview tab lets you see how the source will appear in a report. The source citations include a citation detail field. Citations can be attached to most data (name, events, facts, marriage, marriage events) or at any point in a note. Sources may be viewed, added or edited from the master source list. Database-wide custom log files can be used to track research progress.

Various lists are available and you can mark individuals, lines, ancestors and descendants. An advanced 'mark groups' function can be used to build lists for reports or export and to mark/unmark using a one to four condition filter. Many preset groups have already been defined.

All data from GEDCOM import not going into one of the available or newly imported fields is saved in the notes fields. Delimited text or Generation family files can be imported. In addition to GEDCOM export, data can be exported into a delimited file for spreadsheet/database use.

The Generations output menus are separated into reports, charts and Internet. Some reports may be generated in normal (existing data) or questionnaire (data plus blanks for missing data) styles. Blank person and family group sheets may be saved. A separate charting program, 'EasyChart', is used for elaborate graphical charts that can include pictures. Textual publishing can be accomplished with the family history report or the register report. Reports can be saved as text or RTF files for further editing. Specifying your word processor opens the report in that program. A variety of reports and charts can be generated as HTML files for Web pages and space is available on the www.myfamily.com Web site.

The 'save a copy' function saves a copy of your database to a specified location.

Family Tree Maker

Family Tree Maker is a 32-bit application that runs under the Windows operating system.

A person's preferred name, birth, death and burial facts are entered on the Family Page and are linked to fields on the More About – Facts screen. Unlimited facts for an individual including name variants can be entered on the Facts screen. Each pre-defined or custom fact has fields for fact name, date and a 256-character

comment or location detail. Alternative or conflicting facts can
be recorded and the preferred alternatives marked. Facts can be
sorted alphabetically or chronologically. If fact text won't fit into the
comments/location field, the text is added to the person's notes field.
Some information is recorded on other screens (title, alias, address,
medical information, etc.). Each marriage has a Facts screen where
marriage (or other facts linked to both spouses) and marriage status
are recorded and a Notes screen. Other parents for a child can be
added with the Other Parents option and the nature of the relationships is shown on the lineage screen. Unlimited multimedia objects
can be linked to an individual with the 'scrapbook'.

One or more sources can be linked to each fact, but there is no
way to link sources to text in the notes fields or to fields on the other
screens. Source citation screens for each fact include citation details
and the footnote used in narrative reports. Source screens include
source details and fields for source location and quality.

Research progress and tasks are recorded in the Research Journal,
which can be sorted in one or two columns and printed. Family Tree
Maker can import GEDCOM files, older Family Tree Maker files and
PAF 2.x/3.0 files. It can export several versions of Family Tree Maker
and GEDCOM files.

Only basic search and selection tools are included but a variety of
list reports using subsets of the complete file and custom reports can
be generated. As would be expected, a variety of narrative reports
and charts can be printed. The 'trees' include a unique hourglass tree
showing both an individual's ancestors and descendants and an
all-in-one tree. Publication tools include three styles of genealogy
report and a 'family book'. Several narrative reports can be exported
to text or RTF files for editing. Family Tree Maker includes tools for
publishing to the Internet and space is available for users on the
Family Tree Maker Web site.

Family Tree Maker creates backup files in the location of your
choice and can span multiple floppy disks as required.

Ultimate Family Tree

This is a 16-bit FoxPro application that includes 32-bit components
requiring the Windows operating system.

Ultimate Family Tree, based on its feature set, is the most
complex program considered here. The Individual Record screen
shows name, attributes (sex, living), relationships and events.
Buttons lead to more information (names/flags, miscellaneous,
medical and media), text (bibliographical, footnote and research)

and evidence. It has two editing modes, normal and advanced (with additional data items). Unlimited predefined or custom events can be added. The Event edit screen has fields for date, sort date, place, details, flags, connected individuals with their roles and text (text, footnote, research). The event and most other fields have evidence buttons. Places include custom place levels, each with evidence. A role template determines how each role will appear in printed reports. The template can be edited and the sentence previewed. Additional parents are entered using an event tag such as 'adoption' and the roles of all connected individuals can be recorded. The media options allow you to enter any common media type (image, sound or video) to the multimedia database. Media can be documented and linked to any individual or event.

Evidence is recorded from the Proof screen where you link sources, set CDO (consistency, directness and origin) and enter text (citation details), evaluation, surety, and footnotes. From the source record, you can enter source details and miscellaneous information including the repository and a transcript. The source details are based on pre-defined or custom source templates, each using appropriate components to construct forms for footnotes and bibliographic citations. Ultimate Family Tree includes source templates and specific templates for UK sources.

Numerous lists and extensive search tools using multiple criteria and Boolean logic can be used to find just about any data and to build lists of individuals for export or reports. For example, individuals can be searched for using fifteen different criteria. Individuals may be marked with up to ten flags and events with three flags.

In addition to individual and event research notes and sticky notes attached to windows, tasks can be linked to individuals, events, places, sources and media items. The Task List includes a calendar, task details, progress indicators and repository. Specific reports may be generated such as a task list for a planned repository visit.

Ultimate Family Tree can import or share data with some older pieces of family history software. Data can also be imported and exported using several GEDCOM versions. Data for a group of people such as census records can be entered from a spreadsheet-like interface and the data will then be linked to all of those individuals' records.

Ultimate Family Tree can generate a huge variety of reports with screen preview before printing. Most reports can be sent to RTF files and list reports can be exported as text, spreadsheet or database files. The RTF reports can be edited with Ultimate Family Tree's built-in editor or your word processor and can include table of contents, footnotes, endnotes, indexing and embedded images and objects for genealogical book construction. The list reports can be sent, for example, to the spreadsheet of your choice. Ultimate Family Tree can produce and preview family journal or box chart instant Web pages and can upload these pages to user space available on the Ultimate Family Tree Web site.

Ultimate Family Tree includes a backup/restore utility to selectively backup the various data components (project, library, media, support, dictionary).

SOFTWARE FOR MACINTOSH

Reunion

This software requires a minimum of 2 MB of hard disk space. Reunion shares its own origins (or roots) with the PC software Generations Family Tree, and consequently shares many of that software's features, described earlier. Reunion is a complete, elegant, robust and flexible genealogy software program for the Macintosh. It produces high-quality charts and other types of document. Some of its main features are the creation of large graphic tree charts including descendant charts up to ninety-nine generations and pedigree charts up to thirty-five generations. It also permits GEDCOM import and export. Other facilities include the production of comprehensive listings, which could support the writing of family histories. Full on-screen editing of box colour, font, font size, shadow, border, connecting lines and captions is permitted. A large variety of reports and forms is offered. Reunion provides index, event calendars, family group sheets, family histories, register reports, *Ahnentafel* reports, person sheets, questionnaires, mailing lists, birthday lists and much more. It permits storage of up to 30,000 characters of text per person, in note format.

Personal Ancestral File (PAF)

The Church of Latter-day Saints (LDS) in Salt Lake City used to produce Personal Ancestral File (PAF) in a Macintosh version. PAF 2.3.1, the latest in the 2.x series, is still available for purchase but no future upgrades will be created for the Macintosh system. It is well documented and packaged. It has many features for ensuring that you are consistent in spelling names of persons and places. It can also produce innumerable charts, diagrams and reports. However, the Macintosh version lacks the multimedia and Web site facilities of the version for the PC.

Many of the pieces of software described above have a variety of versions, perhaps described as 'Deluxe' or 'Grande Suite'. Be wary of some of these more expensive versions – at extra expense to you they may contain a large number of CDs of additional census information and other records which may be of very little value to you, especially if the CDs contain information pertaining only to the USA or Canada. More helpfully, you may see some offered for sale marked as 'UK Version' or 'European Edition'.

With any one of these PC or Macintosh family history software programs and properly disciplined work habits, a person could do a reasonable job of recording and documenting their family history. The more sophisticated programs give a researcher more choice over their data recording and more control over report output, at the expense of an accompanying increase in program complexity and a steeper learning curve.

For a more comprehensive list of genealogical software and also for up-to-date reviews, you could refer to Cyndi's List (www.CyndisList.com) on the World Wide Web.

AUDIO CASSETTE RECORDING

Recollections of an elderly relative can be a rich source of family history, forming a living link with past generations. It is just possible that you may be in touch with a personal recollection of an ancestor who was born 150 years ago. Recollections may be more colourful when recorded as they were actually stated to you – they may be in a dialect which is fast disappearing, the narrator may mimic the way in which the story was originally told, and a whole lot of narrative colour can be added to an otherwise fairly sterile piece of family history.

VIDEO RECORDING

Local history
If you are able to visit the area from which your ancestors came, then the use of a camera, or better still a video recorder, can capture the feeling of those surroundings. An illustration of a house where someone lived, the village, the local church, prominent buildings,

local occupations and, for the more morbid amongst us, gravestones can enliven your family history when you prepare it for consumption by other interested parties.

Family gatherings
If a family gathering is held, it can be quite enlightening to record members attending, especially if it is a large gathering covering a number of generations and involving quite distant cousins. Family characteristics can be noted in reviewing the tape, and shared characteristics between groups of family members can be linked with photographs and recollections of particular significant ancestors.

PRESERVATION OF MATERIALS

The original materials which you have assembled, your source materials, are the most valuable assets in your collection. Upon these the construction of your family tree and history will depend; in the light of new source material an expanded or amended history will be developed. Therefore it is most important that you do everything possible to ensure that such materials are conserved in as good a condition as possible – both for your own future use and that of future generations.

Such materials can be considered as archives and can include papers, plans, photographs and other media. There are specific standards for the preservation of archives, such as British Standard 5454: Storage and exhibition of archival documents, and *A Standard for Record Repositories* (Royal Commission on Historical Manuscripts, second edition, 1997). For practical reasons very few private individuals will be able to meet all of these professional recommendations, but attention to some guidelines will help you to minimise the risks of deterioration or destruction posed to your source materials or archives. Prevention is usually better than having to try to effect a cure, and by following basic preservation measures you can help to protect your materials for future generations. Conservation treatments can be expensive, and not all damage is reversible. Features of good archive preservation practice are addressed below under these headings: Accommodation, Security, Environment and storage, Reprography, and Disasters.

Accommodation
• Should be soundly constructed of brick, stone or concrete, with adequate protection against damp or unauthorised entry.

- Should be dedicated to that purpose, as far as possible – for example, not part of a children's play area.
- Should be supplied with a carbon dioxide fire extinguisher, in accordance with the advice of the local fire service.
- Where possible, the following locations should be avoided:
  garages and garden huts
  attics and basements, owing to the risks of water ingress and the difficulty of evacuating them in the case of an emergency
  flat roofs, which are liable to leak
  ground-floor rooms, which are more vulnerable to intruders
  plumbing, drains or guttering nearby
  in excessively light conditions, in the proximity of windows or skylights
  near to gas and electrical appliances, which are potential fire hazards
  near to chimneys, as they may provide a route for damp

Security

- If papers are stored in accommodation which is also used for other purposes, then the cupboard in which they are stored should be locked.
- When tradesmen are working around the area, the archives should be removed or the working practices adapted, ideally under supervision.
- You should control access to your materials, and keep a notebook in which access by others to your materials is recorded. Materials given out should be carefully checked beforehand and on their return.
- You should try to ensure that the materials are fully covered by any domestic intruder alarm system.

Environment and storage

In addition to providing sound and secure accommodation, archive materials also require a stable environment and suitable storage conditions if their safety is to be assured. Over a period of years, unsuitable environments have proved to be a main cause of damage to archives. If the environment is too dry, the documents may become brittle; dampness and poor ventilation may encourage the growth of mould; high temperatures may speed up the deterioration process. In general, a consistent cool atmosphere with adequate ventilation is desirable.

- It will be most likely that your collection of materials will include a mixture of paper, photographs and other media and should be stored between 13 and 18 degrees centigrade and 55 and 65 per cent relative humidity. Temperature and humidity swings are potentially damaging.
- Where there are windows or skylights, the damaging effects of light can be reduced by use of blinds or shutters.
- Shelving should be adjustable and at least 15cm above the ground, and away from windows and external walls owing to the risk of water penetration.
- Papers should be stored in suitable archive boxes. Metal deed boxes are not recommended as they are heavy, liable to rust and will retain water in the event of flooding.
- Volumes should be put on the shelves either upright or flat, never on their fore-edges.
- Separate protection (for example wrapping in acid-free paper) should be given to outsize volumes, documents and maps
- Loose photographs should be boxed and, where possible, put in polyester sleeves.
- Inspect the store regularly for signs of water penetration, mould growth, insect infestation and so on.
- Keep the storage area clean and free of waste and rubbish, as dust and organic materials provide an ideal environment for vermin, insects and mould.
- Don't put original documents on permanent display, either in frames or cases, as this can lead to irreversible brittleness and fading.

Reprography
It is essential to maintain a copy of your most important documents and materials. Despite all the most careful precautions, damage can occur.

However, **photocopying** may physically damage or fade archives. The following types of material should never be photocopied:

- fragile or damaged documents
- parchment
- outsize documents and volumes
- original photographs
- documents with seals attached
- tightly-bound volumes
- volumes with decorative or historical bindings

Photography on your own premises is usually a suitable alternative to photocopying, and will provide a negative for future use. The details are a bit technical for the amateur photographer, but nevertheless lighting guidance is crucial, as follows:

• Lighting should not exceed 1,000 lux, under tungsten lighting.
• If metallic halide lamps are used, this may be increased to 2,500 lux.
• Flash photography is acceptable under certain circumstances: the upper limit for flash photography is 20 lux-minutes or f22 on 100ASA film or equivalent.
• A UV filter over each flash is desirable.

It is important to remember that copyright issues must be respected.

Disasters
• Take increased precautions during periods of increased risk, such as building renovation and bad weather.
• Turn off and/or disconnect all inessential utilities when the premises are unoccupied.
• Arrange comprehensive insurance for the costs of salvage and conservation for your archives.

In the unfortunate event of a disaster you should remain calm and take no risks. Some pointers, while still prioritising your personal safety, are as follows:

• Protect all papers at risk but as yet undamaged with polythene sheeting or move them to another secure location.
• Establish a sorting area for your salvaged material.
• Clear papers that have fallen on the floor first.
• When clearing shelves, start at the top and work down for safety reasons.
• Where possible, remove materials from the storage area in order; if reference numbers are used, evacuated archive material should be labelled with such. If you must write on an original document, use a soft (2B) pencil, not ink.
• Do not attempt to stack boxes if they are wet, as they may disintegrate, causing damage to the contents.
• Remove and replace all damaged boxing. Check first to find out if the contents need drying, as re-boxing damp material will cause serious mould problems in a short period of time, leading to the loss of papers.

- Affected material should be laid out to dry on absorbent paper. Where necessary, clean blotting paper should be used to dry individual documents or placed between the leaves of damp volumes.
- Wet items should be treated within forty-eight hours to avoid mould growth.
- In the event of extensive water damage, wet items (excluding photographic material) may be frozen in a domestic freezer. This action should prevent further deterioration in the documents before they can be assessed by a professional conservator.

Books
- Do not attempt to open or close wet books.
- Damp books can be dried by cold air from fans after being opened and stood on end. Check periodically, and turn them head to tail to prevent sagging and damage to bindings.

Bundles, loose papers and files
- Where masses of papers are found stuck together, there should be no attempt to separate them, as this will lead to removal of print.
- Do not attempt to flatten folded items, as this will lead to tearing.
- Some single-leaf items may be suitable for air-drying.

Photographic material
- Wet photographs will begin to disintegrate and develop mould if left in piles. Wherever possible, air-dry them. Lay out photographs (including glass plates) on absorbent paper, emulsion side up for air-drying. Seek expert advice as soon as possible.
- Water-damaged microforms should be immersed in buckets of clean cold water until they can be reprocessed.

A photographic record of your affected archive material can assist when negotiating claims with your insurers.

If all such measures have failed or you receive material in a damaged condition, the National Archives of Scotland's Conservation Unit can be contacted to advise on commercially available conservation services.

CASE STUDY

Figure 2.1 below may give you an idea of the kind of information you may wish to collate by means of a word processor. It shows information about an ancestor's military record collected from a variety of family recollections, sources and documents.

The Service Record of John Ramsay Winch:

No. 2204213

From	To	Rank	Details
7 February 1903	3 April 1908		Imperial Yeomanry or Voluntary Force: Forth Division Sub-Marine Miners RE
1 August 1904	28 Feb 1909	2nd Crpl	Forth Division RE (Vol.) Electrical Engineers
1 March 1909	16 August 1909	Corpl	
17 August 1909	16 May 1911	Sergeant	
17 May 1911	31 Dec 1913		Renfrewshire (F) RE
1 January 1914		CSM	

Embodied Service

From	To	Rank	Details
5 August 1914			406th Field Company RE
4? August 1914	17 Dec 1915		Home Forces
18 Dec 1915	25 April 1916		British Expeditionary Force – Egypt
26 April 1916			British Expeditionary Force – France
7 November 1917			'Specially mentioned' in Sir Douglas Haig's Despatch, *London Gazette*
2 December 1917			Ph II Order No. 2, gassed
17 June 1918			Meritorious Service Medal, *vide London Gazette* d. 17/6/18
21 June 1919	25 June 1919		5th Prov. Company No. 27
26 June 1919	12 August 1919		Home Forces
9 September 1919			Disembodied on demobilisation at Chatham
31 March 1920			Discharged on demobilisation, para 392 (XXVIII) KR

Re-enlisted Service

From	To	Rank	Details
13 April 1921			'F' (Hld) Renfrew Field Company RE
31 May 1921		Instr'r	Discharged on enlistment in the Regular Army on appointment as Instructor
1 June 1921		Sapper	51st The Highland Division (T) RE
2 June 1921		Sergeant	Promoted authy ACS 337/21 to GOC 51st (Hld) Division A1/835 on 23/4/21
28 August 1922		A/CSM	Warrant Officer Class II
30 March 1923			Service for one year approved
8 May 1924			Service for a further period of one year approved
8 May 1925			Service for a further period of one year approved
11 February 1926			Service for a further period of one year approved
....			Left Drill Hall, joined RE 'Old Comrades'
1929			Clasp to Territorial Efficiency Medal
1939	1945		Home Guard, Bomb Disposal Squad, on disbandment made up to Lieutenant

Alternatively, you may find it easier to use a spreadsheet (such as Microsoft Excel) if your information more readily falls into categories which have fairly brief descriptions, such as the table of Newhaven fishing vessels shown in figure 2.2.

Figure 2.2 Example of information recorded in a spreadsheet

Reg.No.	Name	Date	Description	Other Details
LH 82	May Queen	1887	Steam Screw Schooner	
LH 190	Perseverance	1900	Decked Mainsail, Jib & Foresail	Nets, N/L dredge
LH 749	Joan	1886	O/B Lug Sail	
LH 781	Three Sisters	1886	O/B Lug Sail, 25ft, 5 tons, 5 crew	reg 1875
LH 874	Two Sisters	1886	O/B Lug N/L, 5 tons, 3 crew	reg 1877
LH 909	Hope			
LH 978	Reaper		Clinker 2/Lug, 47ft, 6 tons, 4 crew	motorised 1921
LH 985	William & Margaret		27ft, 5 tons, 4 crew	reg. after engine 1920/23
LH 210	The Reliance	1928	Last boat built in the Fisherman's Park, Newhaven	

To keep your family tree in some organised form, you may wish to use a piece of software specifically designed to keep track of the relationships and links between generations of your family tree, together with some details of dates and other 'structural' information. Figure 2.3 is an example of a screen of information from a specific piece of family history software (or genealogical database – in this case Reunion for Macintosh), showing some more structural information from the family in the preceding examples. You will notice that the information on this 'card' is in a structured and summary form related primarily to births, marriages, deaths and occupations.

On the other hand, more detail of different types of information (such as an army record or medals) can be included in the word-processed or spreadsheet document. The purposes of both are complementary to each other, the family history software providing a means of maintaining and updating the correct links and order across the generations as research progresses.

Figure 2.3 An 'information card' from a family history software program.

Henry Thomas WINCH		Robert MESSER	
1849 - 1899		1852 - 1931	
Margaret Thomson RAMSAY		Jane ROBERTSON	
1859 - 1923		1851 - 1930	

Grandfather   26 Jun 1906, St Cuthbert's Parish Church, Edinburgh   Grandmother

John Ramsay WINCH		**Euphemia Galloway Robertson MESSER**	
Birth	8 Nov 1883	Birth	21 Oct 1875
	Queenborough, Kent, England		13 Ponton Street, Edinburgh, Scotland
Death	6 Jan 1963 Age: 79	Death	3 Mar 1965 Age: 89
	36 Windsor Crescent, Paisley, Scotland		36 Windsor Crescent, Paisley, Scotland
Occ	Company Sergeant Major, Royal Engineers - 406 F	Occ	Housewife
Educ		Educ	
Reli	Episcopal Church	Reli	Episcopal Church
Note	He received 5 or 6 medals in World War 1, namely:	Note	
	Meritorious Service Medal - 17 June 1918, in London Gazette		
	Territorial Force Efficiency Medal (clasp in 1929)		
ID: 13	Changed: 8 Feb 2003	ID: 14	Changed: 15 Jan 2000

| Jean Ramsay | | Marguerite Thomson | |

| Henry Thomas | | Robert Messer | |

10

CHAPTER 3

BASIC SOURCES FOR FAMILY HISTORY

In this chapter we seek to help you to find more information about
your family history, once you have exhausted all the sources you have
available in your family. At this stage the next step is to look into the
documentary evidence available in official documents. The most
important store of information for the beginner in family history
research is New Register House. Based at the east end of Princes
Street, Edinburgh, New Register House contains the official Scottish
Civil Registers, the census returns for 1841 to 1901 and the 'Old' Parish
Registers. It is now also possible to access some of this information
by means of the Internet, at www.scotlandspeople.gov.uk, and the
1881 British census is available on CD-ROM.

BIRTHS, MARRIAGES AND DEATHS
SINCE 1855

If you were born in Scotland one of your parents probably registered
your details with the local registrar. A very similar system applies to
marriages, whether the ceremony is carried out in a church or in a
registry office, and also to deaths.

Since 1 January 1855 in Scotland, the state has assumed responsibility for the logging of the births, marriages and deaths of its citi-
zens. The outcome of all this bureaucracy has been that a vast store
of all the original entries since then has been indexed, maintained
and made relatively accessible to you, as a member of the general
public, for a reasonable fee.

Before we tell you of the procedure for gaining access to this treas-
ure trove of information, we will give you a few notes on what each
type of certificate contains, and what to look out for when you get to
look at the actual entries.

The **birth certificate** will give you, in addition to the details you
already know about the person's name and sex:

- The date and place of birth – even down to the time of the baby's delivery. You should make special note of the address – later on when we look at census returns, you will see that it can be a link to other interesting information.
- The parents' details – names, the father's occupation, the mother's maiden name, and the really valuable information about the date and place of the parents' marriage.
- The name of the informant. This is not normally of importance as it is usually the father or mother. However, if it is not, take a note of it as it may point to a relative and come in useful in later research.

If you happen to have a birth in 1855, you have struck lucky as it will provide you with information about the number of other children of the marriage at the time of the birth, together with the age and birthplace of the father and mother. Because of the burden of collecting this extra information, this practice was, unfortunately for the family historian, dropped after one year. The reaction against this was particularly sharp between 1856 and 1860, as birth certificates did not include details of the parents' marriage. However, this valuable information was reintroduced in 1861.

The **marriage certificate** will be even more fruitful as it contains information about two people, as follows:

- Where and when the marriage took place. If the ceremony was a religious one, it will tell you by which rites it was performed. This is not something to gloss over – it may point to a family tradition of church-going which could open up other sources of information later on.
- The name, occupation, 'condition' (bachelor or widower), age and address of the bridegroom. Additionally it provides the name and occupation of the father, and the name and maiden name of the mother, absolutely vital information to take a step back to the previous generation in your family tree.
- The equivalent details for the bride.
- The names of the witnesses to the signing of the marriage register. Most of the time this will be of little practical use, but take a note of them as it could be a clergyman or a friend or relative of the bride or groom. You never know when this will provide a key to your later researches.

The Scottish **death certificate** is a very valuable document in building up a family tree, unlike its English counterpart. It will tell you:

- The name and occupation of the person whose death has been registered. Sometimes this occupational information is important as it may have changed from the earlier entries in the children's birth certificates, marriage certificate and so on. Of course, if the deceased was well on in years, the informant may well not be too clear about the actual occupation.
- Marriage details. Again this is valuable information, especially where it refers to a marriage other than the one you had known about previously.
- Where the death occurred. When this happens away from home, the regular address is provided, except for the period between 1856 and 1860. Such addresses should be noted, both from the point of view of simply knowing where the people lived, and to allow you to access census information at a later stage in your research.
- The person's age. This is not always accurate, but can be a reasonable guide to enable you to trace a birth entry in the registers.
- The names of both parents, and also the occupation of the father and maiden name of the mother. This information is the vital link which is missing from the English death certificate, and can enable you to take the all-important step backwards in your family tree. However, again dependent upon the age of the deceased, such names and occupations can sometimes be less than accurate.
- The cause of death. This can be a bit technical, but is worth recording. Sometimes the duration of the illness is also mentioned.
- The signature of the informant. The name of the person notifying the death can be more valuable for the family history researcher than the names of the informant on other certificates. It can help you to assess the reliability of the information referred to earlier. Further, it can provide useful genealogical information. For instance, if a Janet Messer (maiden name Robertson) has a death certificate signed by Thomas Meikle, brother-in-law, you can deduce that she has at least one sister, who had married a man called Thomas Meikle – not too bad for a small column at the end of a death certificate.

THE CENSUS RECORDS, 1841 TO 1901

Just as the state had taken over responsibility for keeping track of births, marriages and deaths since 1855, it also became concerned with keeping details of the entire population and keeping track of its whereabouts. Since 1801 in Scotland, every ten years a census of the population has been taken, with the exception of 1941. However, only the statistical details have generally been retained for the censuses from 1801 to 1831, and therefore they are not of much use to the family historian.

The full returns for every household for the seven censuses from 1841 to 1901 are available for inspection at New Register House in Edinburgh on payment of a fee. Images of the 1891 and 1901 returns can be viewed on computer screens, while the earlier records must be consulted on microfilm. Later census returns will not be made available to the general public until they are 100 years old, as they may contain some information about a living person which they would not wish to be released publicly. Increasingly, in order to make access easier, local libraries are obtaining copies related to their own parts of the country.

Census returns perhaps hold the greatest amount of information for the ancestor hunter, but searching through can be difficult. If your family lived in a small village where there were few inhabitants, finding your ancestors may be relatively easy. On the other hand, if they lived in a town or city, it could take an hour or two to find them in the earlier censuses, as they are not indexed by inhabitants' names, and only the larger towns and cities have a street index.

However, the 1881, 1891 and 1901 censuses have computerised name indexes.

WHAT CAN YOU GLEAN FROM CENSUS RETURNS?

In **1841**, the census asked for a limited amount of information – names, approximate ages rounded down to the nearest five years, occupations, and whether the person was born in the county or not. For those under the age of 15, allegedly exact ages are given.

In **1851**, questions being asked were names, relationships to the person designated as 'head of the household', precise ages and the actual parish of birth, if in Scotland.

By the time we reach **1891**, a number of extra and quite revealing questions were being asked, such as the ability to speak Gaelic, the number of rooms being shared by families, and evidence of disabilities.

The big benefit which the census returns bring to the family history researcher is to provide complete or partially complete family groupings in the one place. This could enable you to find brothers and sisters and perhaps other relatives. However, the absence of one expected person is no guarantee that they are deceased – they could have been away from home on business or staying with a friend on that particular census night! The census return will also provide you with information on the social circumstances of your ancestors. Don't neglect to take a look at the details of the neighbours. It may be useful to note down who is sharing a front door, or a close, with your ancestors, or living in the neighbouring farm. Census returns can tell you a lot about the activities of a locality.

SOME PITFALLS

One drawback of census returns is that you must know exactly where your family was living on that one night once every ten years, and you may end up on a long and perhaps fruitless search if your family was quite mobile. The numbering of streets was sometimes a bit disorganised, and different census enumerators could show different standards of care in noting down street numbers.

Figure 3.1 is an example of a census return from our own research.

Figure 3.1 Example of an 1881 census return for North Leith.

(Census for North Leith, 1881 – CEN 1881, 692(1))
26 James Place, Newhaven

Name	Position	Status	Age	Occupation	Birthplace
John Ramsay	Head	Married	48	Fisherman	Born Newhaven
Maryann Ramsay	Wife		40		Born Newhaven
John Ramsay	Son		22	Fisherman	Born Newhaven
William Ramsay	Son		4	Scholar	Born Newhaven

This census entry revealed a hitherto unknown son, of age 4. There is also the possibility that this was an illegitimate grandson of one of the daughters of the family, as such arrangements to cover up a family 'disgrace' were not unknown at the time.

The interesting social background provided by the detail contained in the 1891 census can be seen in the extract from one address shown in figure 3.2.

Amongst other things, the living conditions, particularly of the Shaw family – ten people living in a three-roomed house – are worthy of note as an interesting insight into the social history of the area in which your ancestors were living.

Figure 3.2 Detail for one address from the 1891 census.

Street	Name	Relation	Status	Age	Occupation	Birthplace	Rooms
Williamsburgh 1	HEANEY, Rosean	Head	Widow	50		Ireland	2
Williamsburgh 1	HEANEY, Peter	Son	Unmarried	26	Gardener	Renfrew-shire Houston	
Williamsburgh 1	HEANEY, James	Son	Unmarried	24	Engineer Patternmaker	Renfrew-shire Houston	
Williamsburgh 1	HEANEY, Sarah	Daughter	Unmarried	19	Milliners Shopwoman	Renfrew-shire Houston	
Williamsburgh 1	HEANEY, Alexander	Son	Unmarried	15	Apprentice Mill Mechanic	Stirling-shire Baldernock	
Williamsburgh 1	CHALMERS, Alexander	Head	Married	34	Wood Sawyer	Fife-shire Markinch	2
Williamsburgh 1	HARKNESS, Isabella	Wife	Married	34		Ayr-shire Kirkoswald	
Williamsburgh 1	CHALMERS, William	Son		8	Scholar	Renfrew-shire Paisley	
Williamsburgh 1	CHALMERS, Jessie M K	Daughter		7	Scholar	Renfrew-shire Paisley	
Williamsburgh 1	CHALMERS, James	Son		5	Scholar	Renfrew-shire Paisley	
Williamsburgh 1	CHALMERS, Catherine Herd	Daughter		2		Renfrew-shire Paisley	
Williamsburgh 1	CHALMERS, Isabella Harkness	Daughter		1m		Renfrew-shire Paisley	
Williamsburgh 1	GANSON, Elizabeth	Head	Widow	54	Housekeeper	Ireland	3
Williamsburgh 1	GANSON, William	Son	Unmarried	19	Army Militia Staff	Renfrew-shire Paisley	
Williamsburgh 1	GANSON, George	Son	Unmarried	17	Tailor's Apprentice	Renfrew-shire Paisley	
Williamsburgh 1	JACK, Kate	Daughter	Married	20	Warehouse Worker	East India British Subject	3
Williamsburgh 1	JACK, James	Son in Law	Married	24	Tailor	Renfrew-shire Paisley	
Williamsburgh 1	JACK, Maggie	Grand Daughter		3		Renfrew-shire Paisley	
Williamsburgh 1	JACK, George	Grand Son		1		Renfrew-shire Paisley	
Williamsburgh 1	SHAW, David	Head	Married	53	Power Loom Tenter	Renfrew-shire Neilston	3
Williamsburgh 1	SHAW, Mattie	Wife	Married	52	Power Loom Tenters Wife	Renfrew-shire Paisley	
Williamsburgh 1	SHAW, David	Son	Unmarried	28	Wool Cloth Miller	Renfrew-shire Paisley	
Williamsburgh v	SHAW, Robert	Son	Unmarried	24	Packing Box Maker	Renfrew-shire Paisley	
Williamsburgh 1	SHAW, Margaret	Daughter	Unmarried	21	Housekeeper	Renfrew-shire Paisley	
Williamsburgh 1	SHAW, William	Son	Unmarried	19	Flesher	Renfrew-shire Paisley	
Williamsburgh 1	SHAW, Mary	Daughter	Unmarried	17	Thread Mill Worker	Renfrew-shire Paisley	
Williamsburgh 1	SHAW, Jessie	Daughter	Unmarried	15	Thread Mill Worker	Renfrew-shire Paisley	
Williamsburgh 1	SHAW, Hepsey	Daughter		12	Scholar	Renfrew-shire Paisley	
Williamsburgh 1	SHAW, John	Son		10	Scholar	Renfrew-shire Paisley	

OLD PARISH REGISTERS

As you move back in time in the search for your family roots, you will reach the period before Civil Registration (1855) and the earliest useful census (1841). The most important source for you now will be the Old Parish Registers (OPRs). These are the registers of baptisms or births, marriages, or the proclamations of banns and burials or deaths kept in each Church of Scotland parish, of which there are about 900. There is no standard date when these began and their starting date as well as the way in which they were kept was very much dependent on each individual parish minister. The earliest Parish Registers in Scotland begin in 1553, but only a few date back to the sixteenth century and many began in the eighteenth century. There are some which commenced only in the early nineteenth century and even a few places without any Parish Registers. Many lack burial or death registers. In theory, all the registrations should have been made in the Parish Registers but in practice they are far from complete. Those who were members of other churches, such as the Catholic Church, may not have registered these events in the Church of Scotland registers. Perhaps they will be recorded in registers kept by their own church (see Nonconformist Records in Chapter 7) or not recorded at all. It is always best to consult the OPRs first, however, since many nonconformists will be registered there, plus the fact that they are much more easily accessible and searchable.

Another factor affecting the completeness of these Registers was the huge growth of population in the towns from the end of the eighteenth century. With the movement of population, people's ties with the Church could become tenuous and it was not so likely that registrations would be made. In addition, from 1783 to 1794 a stamp duty of threepence was payable by anyone registering an event in the Parish Registers. This seriously affected the number of registrations made.

For example, John McPhail and Florence McArthur were married in 1787 at Glasgow High Church, but Florence's baptism does not seem to have been recorded, although her brother Duncan's baptism appears in 1773. We know from his will that he had several other brothers and sisters, but only some have been traced in the OPRs.

When considering the amount of information found in the Parish Registers, the first thing to say is that there is normally a good deal less than you would have found in the Civil Registers. Baptisms are likely to give the name and date of baptism of the child, his parents' names, their residence and possibly the father's occupation.

Marriage entries usually refer to the proclamation of marriage which was made in the parishes of both the bride and groom. It is possible that more information may be given in one Parish Register than the other and sometimes there is a statement that the marriage did actually take place, with the date. In most cases, the names of the bride and groom, their residences and the date of proclamation are given. Burials will often mention little more than the name of the deceased and the date of burial.

Although this is the information which you might expect to find, it is possible that, in a parish with an interested and conscientious minister, various other details may be included. Quite often the mother's maiden name is given in baptismal entries and godparents' names could be mentioned. Since these were very often relatives, this could be useful. The actual date of birth might also be given. Additional information found in marriage registers could be parents' names and the occupation of the groom, but almost certainly not ages, which is a great pity from the genealogist's point of view. Burials might give the age of the individual, the cause and date of death and parents' names in the case of a young child. If the deceased still had a spouse living, then his or her name could be included, and if they were either a widow or widower, again this might be specified.

Given the comparative lack of information included in the OPRs, one of the major difficulties encountered is the problem of identifying the person you are looking for. Common names, particularly in the towns and Highland parishes, and the frequent use of the same few Christian names in the same family can make it very difficult to decide who is who if there is no additional evidence such as ages or occupations. All you can do in such cases is gather all the information available from every possible source to assist you in making a positive identification.

The searching of the OPRs has been made much easier by the provision of various indexes, including the IGI, described in Chapter 4. You must remember that the IGI does not include burials and deaths. The original Parish Registers are kept in General Register House and there you will find computerised indexes to the baptisms and marriages, but only a small number of paper indexes to burials. The computer index can be searched for the whole of Scotland or by a particular county and there is also a microfiche version available in Family History Centres of the Mormon Church and in some libraries.

Having found a reference in the indexes which seems relevant, you will then need to look at the full entry. You will be given a microfilm copy, since the originals are not normally used nowadays because of the problems of wear and tear. It is disappointing not to be able to consult these documents from the time of your ancestors but as genealogy is so popular now, preservation has to come first.

MAKING USE OF NEW REGISTER HOUSE

New Register House is normally open between the hours of 09.00 and 16.30, from Monday to Friday, apart from public holidays. A comprehensive instruction leaflet on making use of their facilities is produced every year (leaflet S1), giving up-to-date details of charges and procedures for searching amongst the records which they make available to the general public. Having paid your fee, you will be allocated a desk, complete with computer terminal, microfilm/fiche reader and instructions. You will not be permitted to write in pen, as this can permanently damage the delicate original records. For similar reasons, no smoking or drinking is allowed within the building, but there are plenty of refreshment places of all descriptions within a very short walk. The public search room is located under the dome of the building, and it is a bright, airy place to spend a day searching the records.

Preparation before you go is essential. You should try to establish a number of lines of enquiry before you go, in order to make the fullest use of your valuable day beside the records. We would recommend taking a notebook, or loose-leaf binder, filled with some of the skeletal forms we suggest using, contained in Appendix 5.

The indexes of births, marriages and deaths are now all computerised, as are the indexes for the 1881, 1891 and 1901 censuses. The instructions for using these systems are fairly simple and shouldn't prove too daunting. You can carry out a search for a particular birth, marriage or death over all of Scotland or restrict it to certain areas. These certificates are available on microfiche whereas the actual census records are on microfilm.

It is worth noting that there is a registrar's office in Park Circus, Glasgow, which gives public access to the computer index of the Civil Registers. However, the microfiche copies of the actual entries held there only cover the area centred around Glasgow which used to be called Strathclyde Region. Nevertheless, this is a useful addition to the service provided by New Register House in Edinburgh. This office also provides access to the 1891 computerised census index. There is also a similar facility at the registrar's office in Dundee, which covers a variety of statutory records for Dundee, Angus and Tayside, and Old Parish Registers for Tayside.

SCOTLANDSPEOPLE

Access to many of the indexes of the General Register Office for Scotland is available online via the Scotlandspeople Web site, with payment being made by credit or debit card. One payment will allow you to search the indexes within a period of twenty-four hours and to view up to thirty pages, each of which contains a maximum of fifteen records.

At present the database includes the following indexes:

- Civil Registers of births and marriages 1855–1901.
- Civil Registers of deaths 1855–1926.
- Old Parish Registers of births/baptisms and marriages to 1854.
- Censuses for 1881, 1891 and 1901 (the last two with linked images).

It is possible to search on the following in all of these indexes:

- Surname.
- Forename(s).
- Year of registration.
- Event type (birth/baptism, marriage/banns, death, census).
- Sex (male, female, unspecified).
- District.

Additional searches in specific indexes:

- Old Parish Registers indexes – search on county.
- Old Parish Registers births/baptisms – search on parents' names.
- All marriage/banns indexes – search on spouse's name.
- Civil Registers of deaths 1865–1926 and census records – search on age.

It is possible to search for up to five years before and after the year of registration or age typed in, but you will find detailed advice given on the Scotlandspeople Web site on the best ways to search the database.

Copies of the record entries to which the indexes refer can be ordered online through the Web site.

As well as being a boon for researchers outside Scotland, the site can also be utilised by local researchers to prepare a list of references, the full entries for which can then be consulted on a visit to New Register House, thus making efficient use of time spent there. The site is obviously a very useful resource for those unable to visit New Register House but there remains the difficulty of confidently identifying the correct individual from the information contained in

the indexes before obtaining a copy of the full entry. This is where
access to the full entries, which is available to those visiting New
Register House, is a great advantage, enabling further checking at
each step.

1881 BRITISH CENSUS ON CD-ROM

One very significant addition to the resources available to the family historian over the last few years has been the 1881 British Census
on CD-ROM. This includes about thirty million names on a total of
twenty-five discs. Eight of these store the National Index and sixteen
the detailed information transcribed from the census enumerators'
schedules. This is divided up into eight regions covering Scotland (in
two discs), England, Wales, the Isle of Man and the Channel Islands,
but not Ireland. The set is completed by a disc containing the family history resource file viewer. Version 2 of the viewer is supplied as
standard, but at a small additional cost you can buy Version 3, which
provides additional search options.

The co-operative project which resulted in the production of this
set of CD-ROMs was led by the Church of Jesus Christ of Latter-day
Saints and permission was granted by the General Register Office for
Scotland and the Public Record Office for the contents of the records
in their care to be reproduced in this electronic format.

It is a useful source, not only for family historians but also for
other historians. There are various ways in which the data can be
used, but it is our purpose to look specifically at how it might be
used by the study of family history.

SEARCHING

The following searches can be made on either the National Index or
the Regional disks:

- First name.
- Last name.
- Birth year.
- Census place (county or country).

The different additional elements which can be used for searching
on each of the two categories of disks are as follows:

- National Index.
     Birthplace (county or country).

- Regional disks.

  First and middle names.

  Birthplace (town or parish).

  By using 'Neighbours – Advanced Query' from the Search menu.

  Any word in Household entries (useful for searches on street names or occupations). An exact phrase search can be done by placing quotation marks around the phrase.

PROBLEMS

The spellings found in the original census records have been followed as closely as possible, so there may be difficulties with variant spellings of names. This has been compensated for to some extent by the use of standardised forms of first and last names. For example, Catherine is the standardised form for Katherine, Kathryn, Kate and so on, while Hawkins would include spellings such as Haukins and Hockins. A search on any of these variant names would also retrieve the others. There are still some instances when this will not solve the problem, such as people listed with initials rather than full names, like T. Holton, or unusual names that might be spelt differently like Meshec or Meshek.

Ages are often inaccurately recorded in census records but the search on birth year allows for a range of years up to five years before or after the year you type in, or you could leave this completely blank. Sometimes you may find a family you are searching for but one or more children are missing and this may be because they were living away from home to attend school.

Also, census places may not appear as expected. Uddingston in Lanarkshire is recorded under Bothwell, the parish name, although Uddingston and Bothwell were two separate communities.

OTHER WAYS OF SEARCHING

It is possible to browse through the households in the order they were recorded, which could bring up other relatives living nearby and gives a picture of the social history of the area at that date.

You can attempt to track down female members of a family who may have married but whose married name is not known. This should be done on the Regional disks, where it is possible to search on a specific place of birth. This type of request can be successful if the year of birth is known and if the individual was born in a small parish. The search must be made using the place and year of birth along with the first name of the individual.

You will realise that the production of this set of CD-ROMs has made possible so many ways of searching the data which were quite impossible before. If you are searching for an individual for whom you only have a name, date and place of birth, you now have a good chance of locating them by using the National Index. The CD-ROMs should be available in large libraries, but are very reasonably priced for home users.

1881 CENSUS ON THE WEB

There is a version of the census on the Family Search Web site, but at present it does not include Scotland. The search options are also more restricted than on the CD-ROM version, since it is not possible to search on street names or occupations.

CASE STUDY

Examples of the kinds of information which can be gleaned from the baptismal and marriage entries in Old Parish Registers are shown in figures 3.3 and 3.4. These are taken from the OPRs for North Leith.

Figure 3.3 Information from a baptismal entry from
North Leith OPR.

Baptisms in 1824

Ramsay	**John Johnston**, lawful son of **James Ramsay** Fisherman Newhaven & **Margaret Thomson**, was born the 22nd August and Baptized the 2nd September 1824.

Figure 3.4 Information from a marriage entry from North Leith OPR.

Marriages in 1849 – OPR 692(1)/14

Ramsay	John Ramsay Fisherman Newhaven and Mary-Ann McDonald Newhaven, daughter of James McDonald, Sawyer, Granton gave in their names for proclamation of banns.
&	Thos. Wilson, Blacksmith, Newhaven
	John Affleck, do. , Commercial Str.
McDonald	Wm. Brown, Elder
	Procd. 11 and Married 16 November 1849
	Rev. James Fairbairn Minr. Newhaven

From the statutory records of births, marriages and deaths from 1855 onwards and from census information, figures 3.5 to 3.8 show examples of the types of information and the wealth of detail which can be extracted from such records. It should be clear that all these together can be used to corroborate the information therein, while conflicts of detail can serve to pose questions in the family historian's enquiring mind. It is important to bear in mind that ages given to census enumerators may have limited accuracy, and that information provided on death certificates concerning the deceased person's parents is more susceptible to error than information on birth and marriage certificates.

Figure 3.5 Detail from the 1871 census for North Leith.

Census for North Leith, 1871 – CEN 1871, 692(1)

No. of Schedule – 170   Enumeration Book – 16
 8 James Street, Newhaven

Name	Position	Status	Age	Occupation	Birthplace
John Ramsay	Head	Married	44	Fisherman	Newhaven
Ann Ramsay	Wife	Married	36		Newhaven
James Ramsay	Son	Single	20	Fisherman	Newhaven
John Ramsay	Son	Single	17	Fisherman	Newhaven
Margaret Ramsay	Dau.	Single	13	Scholar	Newhaven
Elisabeth Ramsay	Dau.	Single	9	Scholar	Newhaven

Those with a sound knowledge of arithmetic will notice the inaccuracy of the age of the head of the household compared with the birth date given in the Old Parish Register entry for his baptism in 1824 (an underestimate of two years). It is remarkable to note that both his and his wife's ages were quoted in the *1881* census as only four years older than for the 1871 census.

Figure 3.6 Detail from the 1881 census for North Leith.

Census for North Leith, 1881 – CEN 1881, 692(1)

26 James Street, Newhaven

Name	Position	Status	Age	Occupation	Birthplace
John Ramsay	Head	Married	48	Fisherman	born Newhaven
Maryann Ramsay	Wife		40		born Newhaven
John Ramsay	son		22	Fisherman	born Newhaven
William Ramsay	son		4	scholar	born Newhaven

A Death Certificate of 1893 provides the information shown in figure 3.7.

Figure 3.7 Information from a death certificate of 1893.

Name:	John Ramsay
Occupation:	Fisherman
Status:	Married
When died:	22 September 1893
Where died:	22 Auchinleck's Brae, Newhaven
Age:	<u>about</u> 72 years
Father's name:	James Ramsay (deceased)
Father's occupation:	Fisherman
Mother's name:	Margaret Ramsay (deceased)
Maiden name:	Thomson
Cause of death:	*Morbus Cardis,* Cerebral Embolism
Duration of disease:	10 days
Physician:	Dugald McLaren
Informant's name:	Thos. W. Ramsay
Qualification:	Son
Residence:	
When registered:	22 September 1893
Where:	North Leith
Registrar:	

Worthy of note, again, is the inaccuracy of the age, but this time it is an overestimate! However, it is important to recognise the quantity of genealogical information provided here:

- Parents' names – this takes us back a full generation, in this case confirming the link mentioned nearly seventy years previously in the baptismal entry of 1824. Details of the father's occupation and the mother's maiden name are provided by the informant. However, be wary as the informant may not be totally accurate, since it may concern grandparents or people not related to the informant. The fact that they are deceased will allow you to seek prior death certificates for them.
- Informant's name and qualification – in this case it points to the existence of a son not mentioned in available census records.

A Death Certificate of 1906 provides the information shown in figure 3.8 concerning the wife of John Ramsay, who is the subject of the death certificate in figure 3.7.

Figure 3.8 Information from a death certificate of 1906.

Name:	Mary Ann Ramsay
Occupation:	
Status:	Widow of John Ramsay, Fisherman
When died:	4 December 1906, 3.30 a.m.
Where died:	North Poorhouse, Leith
Age:	72 years
Father's name:	James McDonald (deceased)
Father's occupation:	Sawyer
Mother's name:	Margaret McDonald
Maiden name:	Wilson
Cause of death:	Cerebral Haemorrhage
Duration of disease:	2 days
Physician:	G. M. Johnston
Informant's name:	John Burgh
Qualification:	Governor
Residence:	
When registered:	4 December 1906
Where:	Leith
Registrar:	

In addition to providing details of an earlier generation, this certificate provides possible evidence of either a deterioration in financial circumstances or her own health with advancing years requiring her to move to the poorhouse following her husband's death.

CHAPTER 4

SUPPLEMENTARY SOURCES

Now that we have covered the basic, original sources of information for constructing your family history, we take a look in this chapter at some supplementary sources which you may find to be helpful.

INTERNATIONAL GENEALOGICAL INDEX (IGI)

This massive index is compiled by the Church of Jesus Christ of Latter-day Saints (Mormon Church) and, as far as Scotland is concerned, covers births/baptisms and marriages/banns from the Old Parish Registers and the early years of the Civil Registers. It gives the dates of the events, where registered, the names of the child and father (or both parents if recorded) for births/baptisms, and the names of the bride and groom for marriages/banns. As you will realise from the earlier descriptions of these records, there may be further useful details included in the originals, as well as transcription errors, but nevertheless the Index is a very useful and widely used source.

As its name indicates, it covers countries throughout the world and includes several hundred million names. The coverage in England and Wales is less complete than that for Scotland, since the information had to be collected from County Record Offices/Archives and individual parishes, some of which were unwilling to allow the Mormons access to their records. It is now available in several different formats – the original microfiche format, Family Search on CD-ROM and as part of the Family Search Web site. Many reference libraries hold copies of the first and sometimes the second format of the IGI, but the most accessible and easily used version is that on the Web. There you can search for the names you are looking for, the type of event (birth/christening or marriage), the area (country and also by county for England and the year, up to a range of twenty years before and after the year entered on the screen.

Standardisation of first and last names is used, as in the 1881 British Census on CD-ROM, unless you select the checkbox for 'Use exact spelling', an option which you must use if you want to include middle names in a search. It is possible to look for children of the same parents, by entering the father's first and last names, the mother's first name and the region. It is also important to remember that nonconformist registers are not included in the Index and of course deaths/burials do not feature at all since the Church of the Latter-day Saints has a primarily religious purpose for the IGI.

We would emphasise again that the great advantage of this Index is its accessibility and it provides a useful source at least for preliminary investigations which can be followed up by more rigorous searching in the original official records.

GENEALOGICAL DIRECTORIES

Over a period of years, there have been a few publications of this type, such as the annually published *Genealogical Research Directory*. This is perhaps the most important and all-encompassing of its type, with over 150,000 entries submitted by contributors from the UK, USA, Canada, New Zealand, Australia, Africa and Europe.

Amongst other items, this directory contains a listing of each subscriber's interests, and a directory of the subscribers' addresses. Naturally, the larger international directories are potentially of greater value as the scope of coverage increases the likelihood that there will be someone else interested in the same surname in the same geographical area as yourself. It is usually possible to write to the person listed, enclosing some information from your own research and requesting some information from your correspondent's research in return.

By this means, one of the authors made contact with his mother's Hulson family members, of which no living relatives were known prior to that contact made through the genealogical directory. Furthermore, a family history was traced back to the early part of the eighteenth century. Prior to that lucky contact by means of a genealogical directory, the only information that the author knew was his grandfather's name and the date of his death to an accuracy within about five years.

Of course, this is largely a matter of good fortune. Nevertheless, developing an interesting family history is dependent upon the fortuitous tracing of links. It provides a simple demonstration that every feasible and legitimate way of finding contacts should be pursued by the ambitious family history hunter.

FAMILY HISTORY SOCIETIES

There is a considerable, and growing, number of societies throughout the UK. These societies are set up with the purpose of promoting family history research, most commonly in a specific geographical area. Meetings are usually held on a regular basis, with guest speakers, and most societies will publish their own newsletter. Many now have Web sites and newsgroups on the Internet. Members of that particular society can subscribe to such newsgroups and thereby receive regular emails, normally a digest of members' interests, searches for family members, particular questions and replies in which subscribers can participate. In most cases, the society will co-ordinate projects, such as the transcription of monumental inscriptions in its own area.

There are national overseeing bodies for Scotland and England. The Scottish one is the Scottish Association of Family History Societies; the English one is the Federation of Family History Societies which has a location in Coventry. This latter society produces a series of very useful booklets on various aspects of family history.

It is worth joining your local society in order to meet with others who share your hobby. In addition, it can be very worthwhile to join the society related to the local area of your ancestors. Local family history societies have more ready access to some items of particular local interest, and their members, with the benefit of local knowledge, can be very helpful to you in your research.

A relevant address list is provided in Appendix 4.

SEARCH STRATEGIES

Here are some suggestions about the strategy to follow in your researches, based mainly on the records already described.

- Assemble all the information gathered from your family and your own personal knowledge (as in Chapter 1).

The next step is dependent on how far back this information has taken you.

If it has taken you back to 1902 or later:

- Either visit New Register House to search in the Civil Registers, or, if not able to visit, apply for copies of birth, marriage and death certificates for the earliest family members for whom you know the year and place of these events. You might find it useful to search the Commonwealth War Graves Commission Web site if you know of relatives killed in either of the two World Wars, but do not know their parents' names. (See Chapter 5.)

If it has taken you to 1901 or earlier:

- Either visit New Register House to search in the Civil Registers, census records and Old Parish Registers, or, if not able to visit, search on the Scotlandspeople Web site, then apply for copies of relevant records you locate there. You may want to combine these approaches, by preparing a list of references from Scotlandspeople, to be followed up by a visit to New Register House. If you live nearer the registrar's office at Park Circus, Glasgow, or in Dundee, a visit there might be an alternative to visiting Edinburgh.
- Consult the 1881 British Census on CD-ROM if it is easily accessible and you have family details that far back. It would probably be more effective in terms of time and money to search the 1881 Census in this way rather than through the Scotlandspeople database.

At some point, perhaps when you have reached the middle of the nineteenth century, it is worthwhile investigating whether other researchers are working on the same family as yourself. This can be done through genealogical directories, surname lists and members' interests in the local family history societies for the areas you are interested in.

CHAPTER 5

FAMILY HISTORY AND THE INTERNET

The Internet, they say, is the most important development since the telephone. Or is it the wheel?

What exactly is the Internet? A good question, but not a particularly interesting one. The Internet (as future history books will be sure to tell our great-grandchildren) is a global network of inter-networked computer networks.

What exactly is it that gets people so excited about the Internet? Now that's a question worth answering. As well as being a global network of networks, the Internet is a global network of people, ideas and information. The Internet (or 'Net') is – will only ever be – as interesting, useful and exciting as the people, organisations, companies, governments and so on that are connected to it. It is already pretty exciting – but there's plenty more to come in the future.

Talking of the Internet as a single entity is somewhat misleading. Of course, all the computers on the Net are connected to it and (indirectly) to each other, but the Internet that the authors of this book experience is very different to the one that you log on to every day. And decidedly different again to the Net encountered by the person down the road who is forever looking up steam-locomotive Web sites and e-mailing the Seville Orange Growers' Association.

And that is why the Internet is so exciting – like life, the Net is what you make of it.

Using the Internet now is a very different experience to how it was for the pioneers twenty-five years ago – or even two years ago for that matter. Computer hardware, Net access software and Internet Service Providers have changed so rapidly that the online world is no longer the sole preserve of the stereotypical computer technocrat.

As the technological barriers to Net entry came down, so did the cost: the price of PC hardware plummeted and the Internet's culture of free software was embraced with open arms by a computer-using public fed up with paying through the nose to use over-priced programs. Soon, joining the Net became as easy as putting a disk in your CD-ROM drive and letting it take you online.

What of the future? It is not just that we are wary of giving our credit card details online (which is actually a lot safer than reeling them off down the phone), it is just that as a nation we are not committed armchair shoppers. We prefer the hustle and bustle of town centres, shopping centres, and actually handling the goods for ourselves. Unless Web shopping can prove itself to be cheaper, more convenient or more reliable – ideally all three – there is not much incentive for people to shop online.

The World Wide Web – that part of the Internet which provides Web pages as opposed to e-mail – in its current form is still struggling to really convince people to reject the shopping centre for the online mall. The first Web browsers only supported simple formatting of text and images, but now many multimedia plug-ins enable Web pages almost literally to sing and dance. The furious pace of development means today's Web is unrecognisable from the one originally envisaged just a few years ago. In another five years, we'll look back nostalgically at the days when we were worried about giving our credit card details online and fast Net access meant a 56K modem that actually worked.

From PC banking to online shopping to chats with celebrities and vanity publishing, the Internet is already touching parts of our lives that other computer networks do not even know about. Just as nobody could have predicted the massive Internet boom ten or even five years ago, nobody knows what is going to happen tomorrow. Plenty of people have an inkling of what might happen – digital TV, online democracy, electronic commerce and virtual reality have all had vast amounts of development money thrown at them – but at the moment there are more prophets than practitioners.

In fact, just about the only thing we can predict is that no matter how many billions are spent by scientists, governments and multinational corporations, as far as you are concerned the Internet is going to be what you make it.

This chapter does not pretend to provide a comprehensive and future-proof guide to the Internet but simply an outline of the most salient aspects for the family historian. The two facilities of which someone investigating genealogy will be most likely to make most frequent and productive use are e-mail and the World Wide Web.

CONNECTING TO THE NET

You will, of course, have to sign up with an Internet Service Provider (ISP) first of all and ensure that you have a dial-up modem or cable connection to that ISP. Examples of ISPs are AOL, ntl, CompuServe, Freeserve and Pipex – it's a matter of personal preference and balancing the cost of the service against the speed of access and other features provided. Most ISPs will now offer you the chance to have your own Web site. Do shop around and ask other users what they think – it's still a very competitive market. ISPs advertise widely, so it should not prove too difficult to find one to suit your situation.

USING E-MAIL

In order to be able to read and send electronic mail (e-mail) you will have to obtain software which will allow you to receive, read and send messages. This sort of software is widely available and often free, either given to you by your ISP or already installed on your computer system, or collected from free CD-ROMs on the covers of PC or Macintosh magazines. Some of the most commonly used pieces of e-mail software are Microsoft Outlook or Outlook Express, Netscape Communicator and Eudora. These will also allow you to attach other computer files or documents to your e-mail messages. So, you could attach to your message items such as a word-processed family narrative, a graphic file which depicts a part of your family tree, or a digitised photograph.

USING THE WORLD WIDE WEB (WWW)

In order to be able to 'surf the Net', or to browse the Web, you will require other software, known as a Web browser, which will allow you to see Web sites on screen and to follow the links which connect to other Web sites relevant to your area of interest. Your ISP may again provide you with a Web browser as part of their package, or it may have come already installed on your computer system. The two most common Web browsers are Netscape Navigator and Internet Explorer. These both have features which allow you to keep 'bookmarks' or 'favorites' (sic) which save you from retyping the whole address of Web sites which you want to revisit.

WHAT ARE PLUG-INS?

Frequently Web sites will have extra features that you can download to your own computer system. However, this usually requires that you have a particular plug-in for your system. These are mini programs which add particular functions to your Web browser, such as for receiving graphics, audio, video or for downloading and printing document (or pdf) files. The most common of these are RealPlayer and QuickTime for graphics, audio and video. Adobe Acrobat Reader is the most common document plug-in which can read and print pdf document files and this will frequently be of value to the family historian. Thankfully, these plug-ins are usually free. Most sensible sites which require plug-ins usually offer an option to download the plug-in itself for free.

A useful source of advice on how to connect to and start to use the Internet is provided by the BBC on their Web site at www.bbc.co.uk/webwise. This also covers much other information of a basic and introductory nature, including a glossary of technological terms.
We will now address some specific Internet areas and aspects which are of particular interest to the family historian.

MAILING LISTS

Mailing lists on the Internet consist of a group of people, ranging from a small to a very large number, who subscribe (free of charge) to the list. They can then send a message on a topic relevant to the interests of that list. The message is circulated to all the subscribers either singly or as a digest compiled from the messages of a number of members. Depending on the number of members in the mailing list and how active they are, there may be only occasional messages or, on the other hand, there may be one or two digests every day.

There are now numerous genealogy mailing lists in existence, in fact thousands, and these can be a good way of making contacts and of asking specific questions about research methods, sources and individuals or families. Often members of these lists will do 'lookups' for other members, by checking for a particular name in a source which they have access to.

Some genealogy mailing lists, such as GENBRIT, are concerned with research in a particular geographical area, in this case England, Wales and Scotland. Many counties also have their own specialist

lists. Other lists are devoted to the study of a particular surname or
to a topic such as medieval genealogy, royal genealogy or computers
and family history. The best way to find out about mailing lists is to
consult Cyndi's List or RootsWeb, which hosts the vast majority of
these lists. It is probably a good plan to join one or two lists which,
apart from any other advantages, can help to keep you up to date
with developments in particular fields of family history.

FORUMS

Similar to mailing lists are the many message boards or forums. The
RootsWeb site has more than 177,000 message boards, while
GenForum hosts many thousands. These are discussion forums on
individual surnames, geographical areas or topics, to which messages
can be posted asking questions and providing information. While
mailing lists automatically send to all the subscribers e-mails containing messages sent to the list, forums are viewed on the Web with
messages grouped into discussions on particular topics. It is worthwhile to check whether forums exist for surnames which you are
researching. This is another good way of making useful contacts with
those of similar research interests.

COURSES ON INTERNET USE

If you are a novice as regards the Internet and World Wide Web and
you feel you would like to improve your understanding of and skills
in using this technology, there are online training materials available
such as TONIC, produced by Netskills and Beginners' Central. These
will give you some background knowledge and practical guidance in
this area, including the use of search engines.

SEARCH ENGINES

Although we would usually recommend accessing family history
information on the Web via Cyndi's List, RootsWeb and other major
genealogy sites, there will be occasions when these are not appropriate. Perhaps you want to gather as much information as possible of
any sort about an individual, place or organisation. Various Web sites
other than family history sites may have pieces of information which
would assist in your research and help fill in background details. To
attempt to locate these varied sites, you can use one or more of the
numerous search engines or directories.

We should begin by warning you that these are rather 'blunt instruments' for searching the Web and also that, according to research, they only index a small proportion of it. Nevertheless, they can still throw up useful results, so do make use of them. Which search engine to use is often a matter of personal preference, while there are also a number of metacrawlers which combine results from a range of individual search engines. Google and Alltheweb are at present the largest search engines, covering in excess of 2,000 million Web pages. Yahoo, which is also very popular, is strictly speaking a directory, in which all the sites indexed have been categorized by humans. In search engines, all the indexing is done by computers. This means, of course, that although the resources listed in Yahoo should be more accurately indexed, a much smaller coverage of the Web is achieved compared to the search engines. Examples of metacrawlers are Ixquick and Dogpile.

Most search engines operate on similar principles but there are some differences, so it is worth reading the 'help' screens for the search engine you tend to use most, to discover the best ways in which to enter your search terms. This is important because, as we warned initially, it is often not easy to obtain the precise results you are looking for. It frequently happens that a search produces very many 'hits' but many of them are irrelevant for your needs. This can happen when words you have keyed in as your search terms appear in a completely different context from the one you were looking for.

A very useful Web site giving up-to-date information on search engines and directories, including comparisons of how to enter searches and their effectiveness, is Search Engine Watch. It is a good idea to have a look at this first before selecting one or two search engines to use in tracing information scattered throughout the Web.

ONLINE FAMILY HISTORY COURSES

There are online courses available on family history, some being freely accessible and other more extensive courses requiring payment. Examples of these are the online courses run by Vermont College in the USA, some of which include British content, and the free genealogy classes on the Family Tree Maker's Genealogy Site, again partly relevant to the British family historian. For the British researcher, there are some family history guides which can be accessed via the Familyrecords Web site.

MAIN WEB SITES

We have provided a list of useful Web sites in Appendix 3. Here we would like to say a little more about some of these to help you use them.

One of the best resources to which you can always refer back if you do not know where to go on the Web for help on a genealogical topic is **Cyndi's List**. This is a highly regarded site with thousands of links relating to all aspects of family history throughout the world. There is one main alphabetical list of categories but it is also possible to search by keyword.

GENUKI is the principal British genealogy site, covering the United Kingdom and Ireland. There you will find guidance on general topics relating to the whole of this geographical area as well as specific information about smaller areas down to county level. Lists of family history societies also feature and there are many links to other relevant sites.

The **Scotlandspeople** and **Family Search** Web sites are mentioned in Chapters 3 and 4. Scotlandspeople gives access to the indexes of births/ baptisms in the Old Parish Registers and Civil Registers up to 1901, indexes of marriages up to 1926 and indexes of deaths from 1855 to 1951 plus indexes to the census returns for 1881, 1891 and 1901. Online payment is required to use this service. Further major developments are planned as a result of the DIGROS programme. The DIGROS programme (Digital Imaging of the Genealogical Records of Scotland's People) of the General Register Office for Scotland aims to make all the OPRs, Civil Registers (births over one hundred years old, marriages over seventy-five years old and deaths over fifty years old) and census records (1841–1901) available on the Internet. There will be a searchable index linked to images of the original documents, the images being available on the Scotlandspeople site by the end of 2003. More recent records will also be digitised but, for reasons of confidentiality, will not be accessible via the Internet.

Family Search is the family history site of the Church of Jesus Christ of Latter-day Saints and includes the Web version of the IGI described in Chapter 4. There is, however, much more on the site. Under the Search tab, where the IGI is found, there are also the Ancestral File, the Pedigree Resource File and an option to search family history Web sites. These are all relevant to Scottish research but there are also other options which include only foreign data.

Ancestral File is a collection of linked records with pedigree charts and records for family groups which have been submitted to the Church of Latter-day Saints. The Pedigree Resource File is a similar type of database but the records have been submitted by individuals to the Family Search Internet Genealogy Service. In the first of these, duplicate records have been merged, which is not the case with the Pedigree Resource File. These databases cover all periods of time up to relatively recently, but do not quote the sources for the data. The Pedigree Resource File can also be purchased on CD-ROM and this version gives details of sources. Because these two databases are compiled from information submitted by individual researchers, the authenticity of the content can vary depending on the accuracy of each researcher. Contact information is given for the contributors of the information.

The family history Web sites which can be searched from this screen are sites devoted to one or more families which have been notified to the FamilySearch Internet site by users of the site. Again the value of the information on these sites can vary depending on the quality of the research on which they are based.

You will notice that it is possible to 'Search All Resources' from this search screen, but if you choose to select that option, remember that some of the results may not be from original sources and may require verification. As well as the facility to search for individuals, there are other useful sections on the Web site, including Research Guidance and Research Helps. The Research Guidance section provides guidance suited to the geographical area and period you are researching, while the Research Helps give descriptions of types of records or how to find particular types of information. You may find it useful to look at these for any assistance they can provide.

The **Commonwealth War Graves Commission** is the organisation responsible for the maintenance of all the cemeteries and war memorials commemorating Commonwealth servicemen and women who were killed during the First and Second World Wars and has a Web site useful to family historians. Part of the site includes the 'Debt of honour register', where all these individuals are listed. It can be searched by surname and initials and the results of a search also give the regiment and the date killed. The use of initials only for Christian names is not very helpful when you are searching for James Campbell or John Macdonald, but by clicking on a name in the results screen, you can view details of where the memorial to the individual is located and what the inscription is. Sometimes this gives names of next of kin and so could prove quite informative.

The **Scottish Archive Network (SCAN)** has been set up to provide a single authoritative source of information about the various institutional archives in Scotland. We give fuller details later in this chapter on the archive catalogues project of SCAN, and on the testaments project in Chapter 7, but apart from this there is an interesting Web site available. This has various features including a Directory with contact information for Scottish archives and associations, with links to their Web sites where these exist. Another section is a Knowledge Base, with a growing number of short articles on topics, people, places and types of record in Scottish history. Under the Research Tools tab there is a helpful area dealing with the subject of Scottish handwriting, which gives some examples of letter forms and helpful tips on how to read documents.

The **Familia** Web site aims to make family historians aware of the resources held in public libraries throughout the UK and Ireland which can assist them in their research. As well as the names and addresses of all the public libraries in the UK and Ireland, there is a categorised list for each library showing whether the IGI is kept there, what census returns and street directories are held and so on. This can be particularly helpful if you are planning a visit to a specific area to pursue your research.

The **National Archives of Scotland** site gives guidance on the types of record held there and has pages aimed at describing sources useful for family historians. The online catalogue can also be accessed on the site. Here it is possible to search on keywords or names mentioned in the descriptions of the wealth of documents held by the National Archives of Scotland. Since the entries in the catalogue usually include a brief description of the contents of documents, it should be possible to establish which items may be worth consulting, before paying a visit to the NAS. The catalogue will in due course include details of the surveys produced by the National Register of Archives for Scotland.

The **Familyrecords** Web site is a good source for links to the main UK family history sites and also to family history guides.

RootsWeb claims to be the oldest and largest free genealogy site. It includes guidance on how to trace your family tree, the RootsWeb Surname List (RSL) of more than one million surnames being researched by family historians throughout the world, the ROOTS-L mailing list, along with about another 26,000 mailing lists and 177,000 message boards, links to genealogy projects of various types such as FreeREG and FreeBMD and free genealogy newsletters, such as RootsWeb review, which is mentioned again later in this chapter. Finally there is the massive WorldConnect

Project containing family trees submitted by researchers, with a total of more than 204 million names. Various forms of trees are used here, including pedigree charts showing the ancestors of an individual and descendancy charts showing descendants of an individual. E-mail links to submitters are also included. This huge collection is well worth searching for names that you are researching. You may come across information about a family you are interested in, and in particular there may be another hitherto unknown branch of your family recorded, with a link back to one of your own ancestors. There is then the opportunity of trying to make contact with the submitter and hopefully exchange data with a new-found relative. There are a number of places on the Web hosting collections of family trees to which you can send in your own information if you wish.

RootsWeb is one of a network of family history sites run by MyFamily.com Inc., two others of which we should also mention. The **MyFamily** Web site is an Internet community for families, which uses password control to ensure a safe environment. Families can use it to keep in touch using chats and can create family albums, calendars of events and update family trees. **Ancestry** is a subscription-based service giving access to over 3,000 databases which are continually being added to. There is a bias towards US databases, but British sources are also represented.

SURNAME LISTS

As a spin-off from mailing lists for particular areas, there are often associated surname lists which record the surnames, area and period which subscribers to the list are researching. These are available on the Web, giving the e-mail address of the person interested in each surname. The largest of these is the RootsWeb Surname List (RSL), associated with the ROOTS-L mailing list. This list, based in the USA, is a general list dealing with genealogy and family history from any part of the world and for any period and the RSL now contains almost one million surnames. Lists for the various British counties can be accessed through the GENUKI Web site (consult the list of Web sites under the heading 'Surname Lists'). Sometimes local family history societies also include on their Web sites a list of names being researched by their members. Surname lists on the Internet are the equivalent of genealogical directories and members' interests lists produced by local family history societies and can be very helpful in bringing people interested in the same families into contact with one another. Look at any of the lists you think might be relevant. You could save yourself a lot of work and duplication of effort, gain vital clues allowing you to progress further with your researches and make contact with relatives you never knew existed.

PERSONAL WEB PAGES

Personal Web pages are now very common. Many of them are orientated towards family history, since this is such a popular topic on the Web. Individual family historians put their own family history information onto Web pages, thus making it accessible to other family members as well as to other researchers who may find links with their own data. There is a proliferation of this type of site and you should beware of accepting all you find there as totally accurate. It may be, but then again it may not. Assumptions are sometimes made about relationships without being backed up by reliable sources. On the other hand, you may find sites that quote reputable sources and can be taken as accurate. Check Cyndi's List under the category 'Surnames' for these sites. RootsWeb also has an extensive listing of surname pages, just another of the many ways you may find information about your family on the Web by linking in to research done by others.

ROOTSWEB PROJECTS

There are a number of projects in progress which aim to provide free indexes on the Web to important original sources. Many of these are still in the early stages of development and so it is probably worth keeping track of their progress since they may become very beneficial to researchers. Three projects hosted by RootsWeb intend to cover the major original sources used by family historians: FreeBMD, FreeCEN and FreeREG.

The scope of FreeBMD is limited to England and Wales and is an index to the births, marriages and deaths in the Civil Registers from 1837. The entries give the type of event, name, year and quarter, registration district, volume number, page number and the e-mail address of the person who contributed the data. There is now a significant amount of information included on this database, which totals more than sixty-six million individual entries.

FreeCEN will consist of an index of British census returns for 1841 to 1891, but there is a lack of Scottish involvement at present. The first sets of records were loaded onto the site late in 2001.

FreeREG aims to produce an index of baptisms, marriages and burials from UK parish registers and nonconformist registers, although this is also a fairly new project with no Scottish content so far.

Although of no help at present to researchers tracing families in Scotland, future developments of these databases may make them a useful source.

FAMILY HISTORY SOCIETIES' PROJECTS

Some family history societies are beginning to make data from original sources available via the Internet, one particular example being Aberdeen and North East Scotland Family History Society which has compiled a surname index of over 60,000 names from its publications of monumental inscriptions. This can be downloaded from the Internet as a compressed file. Check out the Web sites of any local family history societies covering areas you are interested in to see whether any similar online sources are available.

ARCHIVE CATALOGUES

One important category of Web site is those providing catalogues of archives. Although not giving you online versions of the records themselves, they do help you to locate records which may assist in your researches. Once you move beyond the standard sources described in Chapter 3, it can become difficult to pinpoint the whereabouts of various sources and this is where these type of Web sites become so valuable. Previously, and still for the many archives without an online catalogue, the tracking down of these sources usually had to be done by contacting individual archives. As already mentioned the National Archives of Scotland has an online catalogue, while the Scottish Archive Network (SCAN) has created a catalogue for almost all of the archives in Scotland. The catalogue gives details of the various individual archive collections held by the participating archives so one search will cover all of these collections. If individual archives have their own catalogues on the Web, there are links from the SCAN Web site to these, which give more detailed descriptions of what is held. The SCAN site turns the prospect of bringing together scattered records about a topic, individual or family into a reality. Included on the site are the very large collections of the National Archives of Scotland and the manuscripts held by the National Library of Scotland.

There is another possible means of tracing records not held in the National Archives of Scotland, by using the National Register of Archives database on the Historical Manuscripts Commission Web site. The database covers material surveyed by the NRA and National

Register of Archives for Scotland, consisting of archival material in Scotland, England, Wales and Ireland not held in the national repositories. Although the entries are very brief, they may be enough to lead you to an important source. Fuller details of the surveys produced by the National Register of Archives for Scotland will be searchable on the National Archives of Scotland online catalogue in the near future.

In England and Wales there are two Web-based archive catalogues which you may wish to consult: the Public Record Office and A2A. The first of these catalogues the PRO's holdings which include some records relating to Scottish individuals as referred to later in this book.

A2A, like SCAN, forms one of the strands of a developing UK archives network, the others being AIM25, linking archives in the Greater London area, and the Archives Hub, focusing on collections held by UK higher education institutions. A2A is already providing a catalogue of archives held by over 320 English repositories outwith the PRO. You might just find some useful leads there.

LIBRARIES

There are many publications relating to family history, local history and other topics which you will probably want to consult during the course of your researches, so it is useful to have some knowledge of where to search for these materials. Very many library catalogues are now on the Web and provide a good resource for checking details and locations of publications. There are useful lists of library catalogues on the Web on the BUBL site, but perhaps the most useful for our purposes are the National Library of Scotland, the British Library, the Library of Congress in the USA, which has a strong collection of Scottish material, and COPAC, which covers many of the major UK university library catalogues as well as the National Library of Scotland and the British Library. The CAIRNS service, which can perform a simultaneous search of almost all of the Scottish university library catalogues, is also worth considering. The useful Bibliography of Scotland produced by the National Library of Scotland is available for the years 1988 onwards on their Web site and the Familia site gives details of the family history resources held by local public libraries. Should you find that a title of interest is held by a library far from your own home, it may be possible to obtain it through the Inter-Library Loan service, which you should ask about at your local library.

Some libraries also have extensive collections of manuscripts, particularly university libraries and the National Library of Scotland, and information about these, including catalogues, are gradually appearing on the Web.

E-JOURNALS

There are not at present any true electronic journals on the subject of family history, although RootsWeb issues several electronic newsletters including RootsWeb review. This tends to focus on the USA, although other areas are mentioned, and includes lists of new Web sites and mailing lists hosted by RootsWeb and short contributions but not substantial articles. Probably of more interest is the journal 'Computers in Genealogy'. This is a print-based journal published by the Society of Genealogists but on the Society's Web site you can access useful articles which appeared in the journal more than one year ago. These deal with various aspects of using computers in genealogy and include many links to Web sites. This is certainly a source to refer to regularly, considering the important role that computers now play in the world of family history.

CASE STUDIES

A few examples may suffice to give you some idea of the results that can be achieved using various Web sites currently available.

In researching the Crawfurd family of Jordanhill, the use of the National Register of Archives site revealed the fact that a collection of manuscripts relating to the family was held by the National Library of Scotland. The collection was examined, copies were ordered of some of the material and a family tree was compiled using the information. In order to supplement what had already been found, it seemed worth checking the WorldConnect Project for any information submitted by others researching the same family. Sure enough, a good deal of material was available, bringing down some lines of descent to the present day, and subsequently contact was made by e-mail with the descendant who had submitted the information. This opened up the possibility of an exchange of any relevant material.

Mailing lists tend to include many messages notifying the list of members' research interests in the hope that other members may have the same interests and be able to come up with more useful information. The Suffolk mailing list was notified of an interest in a specific Hicks family leading to an exchange of information. Along with contacts made through the 'Timperley of Hintlesham' Web site, this resulted in an informal group coming together and corresponding by e-mail on family history matters.

An example taken from one branch of this Hicks family serves to illustrate how information can be gleaned from the Commonwealth War Graves Commission site. C. H. Hicks was killed in the First World War; by searching in the Commission's 'Debt of honour register' under Hicks, C. we find thirteen names listed. By checking each of these, the correct individual can be identified. The details provided are quite informative, giving his parents' names and his place of birth. Many entries do not contain as much information, but you may be lucky enough to find an important extra piece of data there.

A final example relates again to the WorldConnect Project. Some time ago a reference had been noticed to the possibility of a relationship between the Howard Dukes of Norfolk and William Shakespeare, quoting the relevant surnames as Moleyns, Whalesborough and Arden. Having spent a little time researching some published material on the ancestry of Shakespeare, information was found about Shakespeare's mother Mary Arden and her family and it was known that John Howard, 1st Duke of Norfolk, had certainly been married to Katherine Moleyns. Otherwise there was no obvious link and this particular line of research was dropped for a time. Revisiting the problem later, the WorldConnect Project was searched for any clues, and clues there certainly were. By searching for Whalesborough and then browsing through the descendants, links were found to Katherine Moleyns, whose mother was a Whalesborough, and to Eleanor Hampden (whose mother was also a Whalesborough), wife of Walter Arden. This pointed to where further research was needed and although the connection between the Howards and Shakespeare has not been finally proved, the research has been moved on another stage with the help of the Web. In addition, it revealed the link with the Hampden family from whom the famous seventeenth-century parliamentarian John Hampden was descended. This led on to contact with the John Hampden Society via its Web site and e-mail, which may eventually result in some of the Hampden family history being made available on the site.

We hope that at least some of these examples have given you an insight into practical ways in which the Web can help you with your research. Try it out. You never know what you might find.

CHAPTER 6

HISTORICAL INFORMATION

So far we have looked only at what could be described as 'genealogical sources', giving details of births, baptisms, marriages, deaths and burials. These record major events in individuals' lives and provide family links. They give us the basic facts from which we can construct a family tree. Of course, these sources sometimes also give us a bit extra, such as the occupations and residences of our relatives, but for our purposes they are important for the genealogical information they provide. If you want to build up a real family history, rather than just a genealogy, you will need to move on to researching what we will describe as 'historical sources'. These record details of individuals' lives through dates, places and activities which are additional to the major 'life events' covered by the 'genealogical sources' and are very varied.

'THE REAL THING': PRIMARY SOURCES

Primary, or original, sources compiled at the period of time being studied are the basis of all research and so we will have a look at various sources, including some listings which tend to cover a wider range of the population than other sources.

VALUATION ROLLS, 1855–

These rolls were compiled as lists of those liable to pay tax on the value of their property (rates) and are arranged by the address of the property concerned. From 1855 onwards there are annual rolls for each burgh and county, listing properties with the names and designations of the proprietor, tenant and occupier and its value. Unfortunately, occupiers of property at a rental of less than £4 a year did not have to be named and only the heads of households were named.

These records, a complete set of which is available in the National Archives of Scotland, can be difficult to search, being arranged by address rather than by individual names. This means that if you are searching for a family in a large town, but do not have an address, you will probably have to hunt laboriously through several volumes which may be oddly arranged and whose arrangement may change from year to year. Sometimes the names of streets changed over a period of years and also the street numbers. Should you happen to be interested in Edinburgh or Glasgow, you will encounter extra problems, although there is a source of valuation records for Glasgow which may provide some consolation. The valuation rolls for these two cities are divided up by parishes, up to 1895 in Edinburgh and 1909 in Glasgow, and, after these dates, by wards. In order to track down the street you are looking for, you could consult large-scale Ordnance Survey maps of the period, street directories, which show the ward numbers of streets, or, for Glasgow, the 1875-6 index of streets, which gives the parishes for each street. After 1912, the valuation rolls for Edinburgh have street indexes. The Glasgow and Edinburgh street indexes are to be found in the National Archives of Scotland. Otherwise, those materials for tracking down a specific street relating to Edinburgh can be found in Edinburgh Central Library and those for Glasgow in Glasgow's Mitchell Library. Some valuation rolls can be found in local reference libraries or archives, but usually only relate to the period after about 1880.

The other source for Glasgow, mentioned above, is the Valuation Roll Index, covering the rolls for 1832, 1861, 1881 and 1911. Available in Glasgow City Archives, this computerised database arose out of a project on housing patterns in Glasgow from 1832 to 1911 conducted by the University of Strathclyde and contains the names of 352,486 individuals who were proprietors or occupiers in Glasgow during this period. Along with the names, it gives their occupations and addresses and is searched by names. A reference number is also given, but the rolls themselves for this period are not held in the Glasgow City Archives.

There are also some earlier valuation rolls, which are described in Chapter 7.

Another similar set of records held in the National Archives of Scotland are those of the Inland Revenue Valuation Office which include a survey of every property in Scotland from 1911 to 1912. This gives the names of owners, tenants and occupiers along with valuation details and there are associated maps with the properties marked.

ELECTORAL REGISTERS

Also useful are the electoral registers, although they have not survived as well as the valuation rolls. Before the Reform Act of 1832 was passed, only a very small percentage of the population was entitled to vote, but from 1832 onwards this percentage increased with the passing of several other Reform Acts. Details of who was allowed to vote can be found in *Electoral Registers since 1832* by Jeremy Gibson and Colin Rogers (1996). Very briefly, from 1832 to 1867 electors in parliamentary elections were male proprietors or tenants of lands or houses. In 1868 the category of male lodgers paying an annual rent of at least £10 was added. Women, although not receiving the vote in parliamentary elections until 1918, were given the vote in burgh council and county council elections from 1882 and 1889 respectively if they were proprietors or tenants. These women voters are recorded in separate registers for local government elections. Obviously, until 1918 there was a considerable proportion of the population who could still not vote, since from 1910 to 1918 the electorate in Scotland almost trebled. For most of the period, in the cities, the names are arranged by electoral wards. Despite this, you may still be able to pinpoint the address of relatives at a particular date, which could in turn help you to locate them in the census returns. The information provided for the period 1832–1918 is the name, occupation, whether a proprietor, tenant or prosperous lodger and the property which qualified the elector to vote. It should be remembered that the elector may not have been living at the address of the property which entitled him to vote.

The registers which have survived are scattered, some in the National Archives of Scotland, particularly those between 1832 and the 1870s, and others in local archives and libraries. The Mitchell Library has a continuous set for Glasgow from 1846 appearing annually, except for periods during the two World Wars. There are separate registers for the burghs and counties. In many cases, a constituency consisted of several burghs perhaps in more than one county, while the registers for the counties are listed by parish. There are also some registers for the burghs among the sheriff court records and other odd registers in some gifts and deposits collections of the National Archives of Scotland.

STREET AND TRADE DIRECTORIES

Other listings which can prove very helpful are street and trade directories which are available mainly for the large cities. There are long runs of Post Office Directories for Edinburgh (annual from 1805) and Glasgow (annual from 1803), with a few other directories dating back to 1783 in Glasgow and 1773 in Edinburgh. Once again the coverage is quite limited, particularly in the early years, and tends to include the notable and well off members of society, those with their own business or trade and those in official positions. Often these directories consist of three listings, one alphabetically by surname, one street by street and another for trades and businesses. Businessmen may be listed under both a business and home address or perhaps they may own several shops, each being mentioned individually. Although mainly useful for researching the cities, there were a few directories published covering the Scottish counties, such as Pigot's directories for 1820, 1825 and 1837 and Slater's directory, which appeared in twenty editions between 1852 and 1928.

These directories can be found in large reference libraries or local libraries in the area the directory covers. The Glasgow directories from 1801 to 1886 are also on microfiche, while you can find the 1787 Glasgow directory at two Web addresses. The first of these Web sites also has the entries for Ayrshire towns in Pigot's directory for 1837.

As an example, here is the entry for John McPhail, who, due to his position as a mail-coach guard, merited inclusion in the Glasgow directories from 1801 to 1805:

M'Phail, J. Greenock mail-coach guard, Old Wynd

You might also be able to use street directories to trace a private resident over a number of years and if they have been listed regularly and are of a good age their disappearance from the directory can be a clue that they have died. Other sources can then be used to confirm this or otherwise. Two unmarried Holton sisters lived together in Uxbridge Road, London, for many years in the early part of this century. By this date, a good number of private residents were being included in the street directories in addition to the notables, business and trades people and those in the professions. As a result, the Holton sisters could be traced year after year at the same address, until the death of Laura Elizabeth Holton in 1919. Another reason why a name which had been regularly included in a directory should then disappear could be interpreted as a move out of the area, particularly if the person was not elderly.

CHURCH MEMBERS

There are quite a number of lists of church members from the nineteenth century or earlier kept in the National Archives of Scotland. Some of these are separate lists, for example a list of communicants, a communion roll or something similar, and include only adults, while visitation lists, examination rolls or catechismal rolls also list children. These were used by the local ministers to ensure that those over a certain age knew the catechism. A record of younger children was kept for future reference. Other similar lists are included in kirk session minutes. Sometimes these give information about parishioners who had moved from another parish and the date they joined the church. It might also be worth checking whether the church had an account book listing those who rented seats in the church, a practice which was quite common at one time. These lists exist for both the Church of Scotland and other churches and local archives also hold this type of material.

POOR LAW RECORDS

Although 1845 saw the passing of the Poor Law (Scotland) Act, this did not bring about a major change either in those entitled to help or in those running the system. Normally, only the poor who were over the age of 70, those unable to work due to disability or insanity, or children who had been orphaned or were destitute were eligible for poor relief. The unemployed who were fit to work received no help for themselves, but their children might qualify. Basic responsibility for assisting the poor lay with the parish in which they were born or had lived for five years.

Parochial boards were set up after the 1845 Act to run the system, but in practice most of their members were the same people who had managed poor relief before 1845. As a result, the records often appear in kirk session records or heritors' records, kept in the National Archives of Scotland. (The heritors were the landowners of the parish.) Where separate records exist for the parochial boards and their successors, from 1894 the parish councils, these are found among county council, district council and burgh records, stored mainly in local archives. A small number are kept in the National Archives of Scotland.

The information provided in the poor relief records from 1845 is certainly better than for the earlier period, giving the age, place of birth and the name and age of the pauper's spouse and children and whether they were living in the same residence or not.

There were applicants who were not successful and often they are mentioned in parochial board minutes, or in a separate list. Should they have made an appeal against the decision, their case would be recorded in the sheriff court records in the National Archives of Scotland.

Particular to the Highlands and Islands were the destitution boards created in 1846 to provide money, meal or work for those affected by the failure of the potato crop. Their records cover the years 1847 to 1852 and are also in the National Archives of Scotland.

There are now several computerised indexes of Poor Law records available, the largest being for Glasgow, which is maintained in Glasgow City Archives. This covers the period from 1851 to 1910 with over 300,000 entries and can be searched by personal names. It can be particularly useful in tracing birthplaces of many poor Irish people who flooded into Glasgow in the middle of last century and is very easy to use.

Glasgow City Archives also have computerised indexes for Lanarkshire and Dunbartonshire covering 1855 to 1900, with another for Renfrewshire in preparation. The Ardrossan and Kilmarnock Poor Law records have been indexed on computer for part of the nineteenth century, being available at the East Ayrshire Family History Society and Glasgow and West of Scotland Family History Society's premises. All the names, not just the applicants, have been indexed in this case and the Ardrossan records are also a good source for information on Irish immigrants.

An example of a different approach is that taken by the Troon @ Ayrshire Family History Society, which is putting a fairly complete version of the Register of Poor Relief Applications for Dreghorn on the Web. At present this covers 1872–9, but is not indexed. Each time period of one or two years can be searched using the 'Find' feature on your Web browser.

OCCUPATIONAL RECORDS

Coal miners
Being one of the main Scottish industries during the nineteenth and the first half of the twentieth century, mining was a major employer, so there is a fair chance that one of your relatives may have been a miner.

The records in which you may trace some information include those of the National Coal Board. These records, also in the National Archives of Scotland, include the records of coal mining companies from before nationalisation in 1947 which date back in some cases to the eighteenth century. Most, however, are from the twentieth century and the details usually just consist of the names of miners with the work they had done and what they were paid.

At one time, many landowners ran mines on their estates and their records may be in the gifts and deposits collections in the National Archives of Scotland.

Railwaymen

Most of the surviving records of the many railway companies which used to exist in Scotland are kept in the National Archives of Scotland. Some of the records of staff give the employee's date of birth and details of the various posts held while working for the company. The best collection of staff records is that of the North British Railway Company and there are also some railway records in the gifts and deposits collections.

To utilise these sources you will need to have an idea which company your relative worked for. Helpful for this purpose is *British Railways: Pre-grouping Atlas and Gazetteer* (1997), which gives information about the companies before 1923.

For a more detailed survey of this subject, have a look at *Was Your Grandfather a Railwayman?* (Richards 2002).

Armed forces

Since the Army and Navy were run from London, almost all the records are held in the Public Record Office there. For detailed information about the many manuscript sources which are held there you should check the Public Record Office Web site or *Tracing Your Ancestors in the Public Record Office* (Bevan 2002).

Due to the fact that these records are kept outwith Scotland, you may find it particularly useful to try tracing your relative in printed sources available in large reference libraries.

Royal Navy

As far as the Navy is concerned, the printed sources only include officers, so are of limited use. 'Steel's Navy List' 1782–1817, the annual 'Navy List' 1814– and 'The New Navy List,' 1839–55 cover this period, but the *Naval Biographical Dictionary* by W. R. O'Byrne, published in 1849, gives more information for all the officers ranked lieutenant and above who were active or retired in 1846. The father of the officer is often listed, making this a very useful source.

As already mentioned, there are many sources available in the Public Record Office, but, as you can imagine, it is much easier to trace an officer than a rating. One of the main sources which lists all the officers and ratings on board a particular ship is the series of ships' musters held in the Public Record Office, covering Scotland from 1707 to 1878. These give the place of birth and usually the age of ratings, but the big disadvantage is that you must know the name of the ship on which your relative served. Fortunately, from 1853, you can trace any naval seaman by name only, in the Continuous Service Engagement Books 1853–72 and the Registers of Seamen's Services 1873–95. Here you will find the date and place of birth and details of his service.

Army
Once again, the main printed source, 'The Army List', first issued in 1740 and then annually from 1754, only gives officers. There are manuscript lists of officers for 1707–52 in the Public Record Office at Kew. Most important amongst the manuscript sources for other ranks are the muster books and pay lists, the main series beginning in 1732. You will need to know the regiment your relative served in to use these records, but if you manage to trace him back to the date of enlistment, you should find his age and the place he enlisted, although not always his place of birth. Another useful series of records are the soldiers' documents 1760–1913, which give details of soldiers who were discharged to pension. These are arranged by regiment (to 1872), then in four categories (to 1883) and finally the arrangement is alphabetical by surname. The information given relates to the soldiers' army service as well as his age, place of birth and previous occupation. After 1883, some additional details of family are listed. These sources are all housed in the Public Record Office.

There are some details of militia amongst the sheriff court and county council records and in some gifts and deposits collections in the National Archives of Scotland and also housed there are some Ministry of Defence records with lists of members of Territorial and Auxiliary Forces Associations. Information on Volunteer Forces can also be found in some of the gifts and deposits collections.

Royal Air Force
Records up until the mid-1920s of those serving in the RAF, formed in 1918, and its predecessors, the Royal Flying Corps and Royal Naval Air Service, are available in the Public Record Office. Further details

can be found on their Web site, while 'The Air Force List', published from 1919, lists RAF personnel.

Merchant seamen

The main sources of information on merchant seamen in this period are agreements made between the masters of ships and crew members before they set sail. Such agreements became compulsory in 1835 and as a result there are various crew lists in the National Archives of Scotland, Glasgow City Archives, the Public Record Office, the National Maritime Museum in London and the Memorial University, Newfoundland. The agreements quote the name, age and place of birth of the crew members, but unless you know the name of the ship to search, or in some cases the port, you will be looking for a needle in a haystack, or perhaps a fish in the ocean.

Businesses

Many records of businesses have now found their way to record offices and in some cases these include records giving employees' names, especially wages books. To see what is available, you will need to check with the National Archives of Scotland, the National Register of Archives for Scotland, the Business Records Centre at the Glasgow University Archives and local archives. The Business Records Centre has a particularly good collection of material for the west of Scotland, while the Scottish Brewing Archive, also held in the Glasgow University Archives, includes records of many companies from the Edinburgh area. One other source available in the Glasgow University Archives is a computer index of bankruptcies for the period from about 1745 to 1914. This index is also available in the National Archives of Scotland, where the original records concerning bankruptcies are held.

If you are looking for information about either the Bank of Scotland and its constituent banks from 1695 or the Royal Bank of Scotland, you should note that they both have their own archives. The Royal Bank's Web site has an archive guide giving details of the records held from the 1660s onwards. Both of these archives include not only the records of the various banks but also some business collections.

Clergymen

Information on clergymen from most of the main denominations can be found in printed sources, the most important being the *Fasti Ecclesiae Scoticanae*. This consists of several volumes detailing the ministers of the Church of Scotland from 1560 onwards and gives biographical and family information about them.

Other publications are listed in the Bibliography. You may wish to look for additional information by consulting the records of the churches themselves or contacting the offices of the relevant denomination.

School teachers

Many books have been written about individual schools in Scotland and so you might find it worthwhile to begin any search for relatives who were school teachers by investigating whether anything has been written about the school or area which interests you. Very useful here are *A Bibliography of Scottish Education before 1872* (1970) and *A Bibliography of Scottish Education 1872–1972* (1974), both by James Craigie, and the 'Scottish education bibliography 1970–1990 on CD-ROM' (Harrison 1994). These list both books and articles and if there is any material on your school or area, the chances are it will be mentioned.

Moving on to manuscript sources, which are in the National Archives of Scotland or local archives, we find a change in responsibility for schools occurring in 1872 when education became compulsory in Scotland with the passing of the Education (Scotland) Act. Before this time, teachers in the burghs were appointed by the burgh council and are recorded in the council minutes. Outwith the burghs, the normal procedure was for the heritors and minister of each parish to nominate a schoolmaster who was interviewed by the presbytery to establish his suitability. Appointments of parish schoolmasters were mentioned in the heritors' records with the confirmation by the presbytery in the presbytery minute books. Since the schoolmaster often became the session clerk, he may also be mentioned in the kirk session records.

The formation of the Free Church of Scotland in 1843 also resulted in the founding of Free Church schools whose teachers were appointed by the deacons of the church. The deacons' court minutes is the source which records these appointments.

The problems of the lack of schools in the Highlands and Islands attracted special attention from three sources: the Government, the Society in Scotland for Propagating Christian Knowledge (SSPCK) and a Mr James Dick.

There are records of grants made by the Government to finance extra schools in these areas for the period 1840 to 1863 and these name the schoolmasters receiving them.

The SSPCK also set up schools in the Highlands and Islands and an alphabetical list of the schoolmasters, with their dates of service, can be found in *SSPCK Schoolmasters 1709–1872*, edited by A. S. Cowper (1997).

Finally we turn to Mr James Dick. In accordance with his will, the Dick Bequest Trust was set up to provide assistance to schoolmasters in country parishes in the counties of Aberdeen, Banff and Moray. The Trust's records begin in 1832 and may prove useful if you had a teacher relative working in that area. These records are also in the National Archives of Scotland.

The Educational Institute of Scotland was founded in 1847 as a professional association for teachers and its records, which are deposited in the National Archives of Scotland, give the names of its members. Within this collection are some earlier records of societies for teachers in Glasgow (1794–1836), Roxburgh (1811–40) and Jedburgh (1824–72).

In 1872 the responsibility for the provision of schools passed to school boards which mentioned the appointment of teachers and pupil-teachers in their minute books. These usually formed part of the county council records and may be kept in local archives or libraries, although a few are in the National Archives of Scotland.

There are some other sources detailed in *Tracing Your Scottish Ancestors*, by Cecil Sinclair (1997), but these tend to cover short periods or only a small number of schools.

Doctors

A considerable amount of information is available about doctors from published sources, namely 'The Medical Register', published annually from 1859, and 'The Medical Directory.' 'The Medical Directory' appeared under that title from 1870 onwards; before this Scottish doctors are listed in the 'Medical Directory for Scotland' 1852–60 and then the 'London and Provincial Medical Directory' 1861–9. This is also an annual and gives more details than 'The Medical Register.' There is often a brief summary of the individual's career, with qualifications, positions held and perhaps references to any published work they had produced.

If you are trying to trace a doctor from before 1858, it may be worth contacting one or more of the three professional bodies concerned with the profession, the Royal College of Surgeons of Edinburgh, the Royal College of Physicians and Surgeons of Glasgow or the Royal College of Physicians of Edinburgh. The first two of these bodies could license surgeons and doctors to practise and have records of licentiates dating back to 1770 and 1785 respectively. In the case of the Royal College of Physicians of Edinburgh, the procedure was different and their licentiates would all have studied at a university. It should be said that these lists of licentiates include little information and the university records could be a more fruitful source for those doctors and surgeons who studied there.

Other medical and related professions

Registers of nurses from 1885 to 1930 are preserved in the National Archives of Scotland and then from 1921 there were registers published annually. Midwives, dentists and chemists can also be sought in published annual registers from 1917, 1879 and 1869 respectively, although these published registers are not easily accessible.

Another avenue for tracing medical workers, particularly those associated with hospitals, are the records of health boards, many of which begin in the eighteenth century. Of course these also include a good deal of information about patients, but being un-indexed could prove very difficult to use for this purpose. Major collections are preserved for Dumfries and Galloway Health Board at Crichton Royal Hospital, Dumfries, for Northern Health Services at Aberdeen Royal Infirmary, for Greater Glasgow NHS Board at Glasgow University Archives and for Lothian Health Services at Edinburgh University Library. The last two have Web sites containing catalogues of their collections, which, as well as the expected hospital records, include gifts and deposits of papers from individuals connected in some way with the medical professions.

Lawyers

Once again, printed sources will probably be the first port of call in the search for relatives in the legal profession. If your relative was an advocate, which meant he could plead cases in the Court of Session, he should appear in *The Faculty of Advocates in Scotland* (Grant 1944). Here you will normally find the name of the advocate's father, the date of his own birth and death and details of any marriages. Solicitors, or, as they used to be called, writers, should be listed in *The Register of the Society of Writers to the Signet* (1983) covering from the fifteenth century to the 1980s although this is not comprehensive. Many Aberdeen solicitors are listed in the *History of the Society of Advocates in Aberdeen* (Henderson, 1912).

The main annual published list of lawyers is the 'Scottish Law List' published for 1848 to 1849 and then the 'Index Juridicus: The Scottish law list' from 1852 onwards.

There are various manuscript records in the National Archives of Scotland but you will probably not need to resort to them for this period. Details can be found in *Tracing Your Scottish Ancesters*.

EDUCATIONAL SOURCES

School pupils
A small number of schools have published lists of pupils and you may be able to trace these in local libraries. Many admission registers have survived and also school log books, recording the day-to-day events in the schools. These log books do mention names of pupils, but apart from this they can provide some anecdotal background information for your family history. These school records tend to date from 1872, but some are earlier and you will normally find them in local archives. Otherwise, there are leaving certificate registers from 1908 in the National Archives of Scotland, listing all those presented for the leaving certificate; however, there is a seventy-five year closure period on these.

University students
All of the four oldest Scottish universities have published information about their former students, some much more extensively than others.

Glasgow has published matriculation albums for 1728 to 1858 and the roll of graduates 1727–1897. The first of these works gives fuller information than the second, usually listing the name of the graduate's father and other biographical details.

St Andrews matriculation registers 1747–1897 and for Aberdeen, the Roll of Alumni in Arts of University and King's College and Marischal College graduates 1593–1860, although published, are little more than lists of names.

Finally, Edinburgh has only published lists of graduates in particular subjects.

It may be worthwhile contacting the university itself, which will probably have some unpublished records.

An example from the Glasgow University Matriculation Albums illustrates the extra information you may find:

1834 AD. 13232 RICARDUS SHAEN *filius natu secundus Samuelis jurisconsulti in parochia de Hatfield Peverell et comitatu de Essex.* Born in 1817. BA 1836, MA 1837. Minister at (1) Lancaster, 1842–5, (2) Edinburgh, 1845–50, (3) Dudley, 1852–5, (4) Royston, Herts, 1855–94. Died 24 January 1894.

Students of other educational institutions

A number of Scottish colleges were founded in the nineteenth century and records of students have often survived. For example, Jordanhill College of Education, now the Faculty of Education of the University of Strathclyde, has student registers from the middle of the nineteenth century, as well as various other sources such as letter books which often mention students. National registers of candidates qualifying as teachers at the various teacher training colleges were published annually from 1857 to 1907 and an almost complete set is held in the Jordanhill Archives, University of Strathclyde.

You should contact the particular college itself to confirm whether any relevant documents have survived and if so where they are kept.

An additional aid to assist the tracing of records of Higher Education institutions is now available in the form of the Archives Hub, a Web-based catalogue of archives held by many of these institutions throughout the United Kingdom.

NEWSPAPERS

Although these can be a very useful and illuminating source, particularly for filling in interesting details about individuals, they are often very difficult to use, given that most are un-indexed. This means some very laborious searching, especially for the most interesting news items. There are also the notices of births, marriages and deaths, and obituaries for well-known characters from the area, which are fairly easy to locate in each issue of the paper, but to pick up news stories, your task is much more difficult. *The Glasgow Herald* has an index for the period 1906–84 and recently a number of projects have been set up to index local newspapers, but the proportion covered is very small. The Familia Web site lists locally produced newspaper indexes held in local public libraries under the category 'unpublished indexes', so is worth checking.

To trace whether there are any newspapers covering the area and period you are interested in, consult the *Directory of Scottish Newspapers* compiled by Joan P. S. Ferguson (1984), which also lists where copies can be found.

THE 'REAL THING', ONCE REMOVED: SECONDARY SOURCES

LOCAL HISTORIES AND FAMILY HISTORIES

Although the original, or primary sources, are the basis of all research, secondary sources such as local and family histories are worth consulting – not only for the possibility of finding specific information about your family, but also to gather background historical information relating to a particular locality or family. Usually you will find a good collection of such works in the local library or in the main reference libraries such as Edinburgh City Library or the Mitchell Library in Glasgow. To investigate whether any histories have been published about the area or family you are researching, consult for local histories *A Contribution to the Bibliography of Scottish Topography* (Mitchell 1917), *A Bibliography of Works Relating to Scotland 1916–1950* (Hancock 1959) and the *Bibliography of Scotland* produced by the National Library of Scotland, covering the period 1976 onwards (from 1988 onwards available on the National Library Web site); and for family histories, *Scottish Family Histories* (Ferguson 1986).

BIOGRAPHICAL REFERENCE SOURCES

You might think it unlikely that any of your family would appear in dictionaries of biography, but since these are fairly accessible in reference libraries and also since as your research progresses you may discover new family names and people of some importance, it is worth looking.

The main reference work of British biographies is the *Dictionary of National Biography*, or DNB. This massive work was published in sixty-three volumes, from 1885 onwards, with three supplementary volumes appearing in 1901. Since then, a new volume has been issued covering roughly each ten-year period, except for 1981–5 and 1986–90. It has also been published on CD-ROM. This work contains biographies of individuals arranged alphabetically, though obviously many other names are briefly mentioned and in the CD-ROM version it is possible to search for these. As a result, the CD-ROM is a valuable asset.

A much more recent production is the *British Biographical Archive*, published on microfiche in two series. This includes entries from several hundred reference works published in the period

1601–1974, but does not include the DNB or *Who Was Who*. It is only likely to be available in very large reference libraries. There is an index to this, forming part of the World Biographical Index on the Web.

The volumes of *Who Was Who* are compiled from *Who's Who* and include many who have not gained an entry in the DNB. These cover from 1897 onwards, with an index volume covering 1897–1990. The annual volumes of *Who's Who* itself begin in 1849, although before 1897 they are little more than lists of names. There is also a CD-ROM version for 1897–1998.

Another work of possible use is *Modern English Biography*, by Frederic Boase, first published in 1892–1921, which, despite its title, includes many Scots. This work, in six volumes, provides brief biographies of persons who died between 1851 and 1900.

Specifically Scottish biographies are covered by *Biographical Dictionary of Eminent Scotsmen* by Robert Chambers, published in 1835, and *The Scottish Nation* by William Anderson (1875), but only fairly major figures are included. *The Scottish Nation* includes information on surnames and families as well as on individuals. There is also the recent *Chambers Scottish Biographical Dictionary* (Goring 1992) but again this only covers the most famous.

If you think you have a connection with the nobility or landed gentry, you should consult *Burke's Peerage, Burke's Landed Gentry, Debrett's Peerage* and in particular, for Scotland, *The Scots Peerage* by Sir James Balfour Paul (1904–14). There are also a number of biographical dictionaries dealing with important figures associated with a particular area, such as *Who's Who in Glasgow in 1909*, or connected with a subject such as science or music, for example, *British Musical Biography*, (Brown 1897).

CASE STUDY

Here is a real example of how some of the sources mentioned in this chapter can be used to research a family's history.

Margaret Conway was left a widow at the end of December 1879, with the unexpected death of her husband James at the age of 39. Having five young children aged 10 down to 1, she was in need of assistance and so applied for poor relief in 1880. This is recorded in the Poor Relief Applications database in Glasgow City Archives in which married women are indexed under both their married and maiden surnames. The original record provides very useful information, giving the age and birthplace of the applicant and the names and ages of her children. Also, to establish responsibility for financial assistance to be given, the addresses at which the family had lived over the previous few years are listed. Finally, and what could be most useful to a researcher, the age of the dead husband is given along with his place of birth, which was Greyabbey in Ireland. This last piece of information could be very difficult to discover in any other way and so provides a very helpful pointer for further research on James Conway and his family. The details of the family's addresses also show how they moved very frequently over this period of time and give us a small insight into one aspect of their lifestyle.

Moving back in time, we know from the marriage certificate of James Conway and Margaret Gray of 1866 that Margaret was living at 33 Green Street at that time and that her parents were Hugh Gray (deceased) and Margaret Gray, maiden surname Dougall. It would be helpful to gather as much information about the family before passing the 'threshold' of 1855 into the period of parish registers and the best source for this would be the census of 1861. By using the valuation rolls database in Glasgow City Archives it might be possible to check very quickly the address in 1861 of her parents, or mother, if Hugh Gray was dead by this date. Sure enough, Margaret Gray is recorded at 33 Green Street, but not Hugh. This address could now be followed up in the census records, revealing further details which help in the search before 1855.

Turning now to street directories, a fairly easily accessible source, we can check through the annual volumes about this period to see whether there are any of our particular family members listed under Gray or Dougall. Here we find in the Glasgow Directory for 1857–8:

Dougall, John, tobacconist and tallow chandler, 15½ Main Street, Calton; house, 17 Green Street, do.

From the next year, he was in business with his brother and similar entries appear for several years and then stop. It had been known that John entered the medical profession, but this earlier involvement in business was new information. Once he had taken up medicine, he pops up again in a new guise in the directory for 1870–1:

Dougall, John, physician and surgeon, 115 Paisley road; house, 119, do.

As you will see, he has two entries, one for his home address and the other for that of his medical practice. He was also Medical Officer of Health for Kinning Park for a number of years and since lists of such officials are included in some directories, he is also mentioned in that capacity in a section on the burgh of Kinning Park.

Although only a small proportion of the population were eligible to vote in the nineteenth century, it may be worthwhile checking electoral registers if these are readily available. In this particular instance, John and his brother Alexander Dougall qualified to vote as joint tenants of 'works', since they rented premises for their small business. Perhaps this might have encouraged an interest in the politics of the day – but who did they vote for? Something to speculate about, but certainly something to include in a narrative history of the family.

Since we know that John Dougall was a member of the medical profession, it is important to consult sources such as 'The Medical Register' and 'The Medical Directory'. Here are examples of the relevant entries in these publications, showing the difference in the amount of detail provided.

John Dougall's entry in 'The Medical Register' for 1876 is shown in figure 6.2.

Figure 6.1 An entry from 'The Medical Register' for 1876.

Date of Registration	Name	Residence	Qualification
1869 May 25	DOUGALL, John	115 Paisley Road, Glasgow	MB 1869, Mast. Surg. 1869, MD 1871, Univ. Glasg.

In 'The Medical Directory' for 1875 we find a much fuller entry, as shown in figure 6.2.

Figure 6.2 An entry from 'The Medical Directory' for 1875.

DOUGALL, John, 2, Cecil-pl. Glasgow – M.D. Glasg. 1871, M.B. and C.M. 1869; (Univ. Glasg.); Sec. Glasg. Southern Med. Soc.; Mem. Gen. Counc. Univ. Glasg.; Mem. Counc. Geol. Soc. Glasg.; Mem. Nat. Hist. Soc., Chem. Sect. Philos. Soc., and Med. Chir. Soc. Glasg.; Mem. Brit. Assoc. for Adv. of Sci.; Med. Off. Health Kinning Park. Author, 'On the Relative Power of various Substances to prevent Generation of Animalculae, with special reference to the Germ Theory of Putrefaction,' Trans. Brit. Assoc. Adv. Sci. 1871–2. Contrib. 'Putrefiers and Antiseptics,' Glasg. Med. Journ. 1873; 'The Dissemination of Zymotic Diseases by Milk,' Ibid, 1873; 'Case of Ovarian Dropsy during Pregnancy,' Obst. Journ. Gt. Brit. 1874 ; various other Contribs. to Med. Journs.

It is clear that John was a graduate of Glasgow University and so we are led to another source – the records of the university. Here is the entry from the Glasgow University Roll of Graduates. Under

Dougall, John we find three entries. The first is obviously the one we are looking for, but the third, John M'Phail Dougall, was a son of the first John Dougall who also became a doctor. Here they both are:

> Dougall, John, M.B., C.M. 1869, M.D. 1871. Catrine; Glasgow (Lecturer on Clinical Medicine in Royal Infirmary; Professor of Materia Medica in St. Mungo's College).

> Dougall, John M'Phail, M.B., C.M. 1880, M.D. 1886. Glasgow; York; Glasgow; Dunoon; Welburn, Yorks.

As you can see, the various residences of the graduates are given. We have now gathered a considerable amount of information about John Dougall and since he appears to be a man of some importance, it is worthwhile checking in biographical dictionaries which include figures of local significance. There is such a work for Glasgow at this period, entitled *Who's Who in Glasgow in 1909,* and there we find an entry, including a photograph, but since he died in 1908 it is a very full entry covering his whole career. His year of birth is given and some details about his early life, including a mention of his father and his mother's uncle 'Sir' Duncan McArthur. Duncan was never actually knighted and some of the other information about him was inaccurate, but it was based on fact. The entry continues with mention of John's career in the soap, and candle-making business and his eventual entry into the medical profession, in which he acted as a dresser to Joseph Lister in Glasgow Royal Infirmary and received notable appointments as Medical Officer of Health for Kinning Park and Professor at the St Mungo College. A good deal of the information mentioned here had already come to light from other sources such as street directories, university records and medical directories, but to discover a biographical notice usually adds a few personal details about the individual which may be impossible to find otherwise. For example, we are told that John acted as a precentor in various churches and also that as a young man he narrowly escaped death when working in Tennant's Works at St Rollox. He rushed into a cloud of chlorine gas at a new bleaching-powder chamber and almost suffocated.

This entry was a great find and if you think a relative of yours might be included in a similar type of publication it is well worth checking. The local library or a large reference library may be able to help you here.

Individuals of this sort often receive obituaries in local newspapers and John is no exception with an obituary in *The Glasgow Herald.*

CHAPTER 7

HISTORICAL SOURCES PRE-1855

In this chapter we provide an introduction to the main sources, other than the Old Parish Registers, for the period before 1855, although some are also relevant beyond that date.

MONUMENTAL INSCRIPTIONS

As a supplement to the records of burials in the Old Parish Registers, it is well worth searching for monumental inscriptions. The information recorded on gravestones is often fuller than in a burial entry, giving the date of death rather than burial and possibly a mention of the occupation and residence of the person. Probably the biggest advantage, however, of finding an inscription from a gravestone is the likelihood that other members of the family will be mentioned. This opens up the possibilities of discovering previously unknown relatives, such as other children or parents of the deceased. Quite often the burial plot, or lair, was used by the family for several generations, so stones which pre-date the introduction of Civil Registration in 1855 can be particularly helpful in establishing family links which are difficult or even impossible to discover in the less reliable church registers.

To find this sort of information, you may want to wander round a peaceful country churchyard in search of your family's gravestones, but in many cases this will not be the most effective means of finding the desired details. The weather has taken its toll on many stones, which have become indecipherable, but, fortunately, a great deal of effort by various enthusiasts has resulted in the transcribing of very many monumental inscriptions. Major collections of these inscriptions can be found in the Scottish Genealogy Society's library in Edinburgh, and in the National Archives of Scotland. Local libraries should also have copies of the volumes covering their own locality.

Although their significance is greater before 1855, inscriptions have continued up until the present day and so should not be ignored as a possible source for the more recent period. Since the work of transcription has concentrated on the pre-1855 stones, it may prove more difficult to trace later inscriptions. Check local libraries and archives for lists. In the cities, there are many cemeteries run by the parks departments of the local authorities. Although they do not record the inscriptions, lists of interments have usually survived, kept either by the parks department or deposited in a local archives office. If you manage to track down an entry in one of these lists, it will probably give a location for the burial, where you can then look for a gravestone and maybe find a mine of information. On the other hand, on arriving at the spot, you could discover that no stone was erected. It is just one of those chances you take in the family history search.

WILLS AND TESTAMENTS

In Scotland in former times, unlike England, only moveable property such as money, furniture and equipment connected with a trade could be bequeathed in a will. As a result, land or houses could not be included and this remained the situation until after 1868. For records of the inheritance of land or houses, see the next section.

On the death of an individual, in theory someone should be appointed to administer the disposal of any moveable property and that person is named the executor. In cases where the individual left a will, an executor is usually named in it, but if there is no will, the deceased is 'intestate' and an executor is appointed by the appropriate court. Both situations require the confirmation of the executor by the court, which is how the transaction comes to be legally recorded. The resulting records are called testaments, either a testament-testamentar if there is a will, or a testament-dative if there is not.

It is unfortunately the case that very few people left wills and even those who did may not have had an executor confirmed, but if you are lucky enough to trace some wills relating to your family you should find them good sources of genealogical and historical information.

The information usually found in testaments is the name of the deceased, date of death, confirmation of the executor, inventory of moveable property and a will if there is one. Supposing there is a will, you might find quite a number of relatives mentioned, but particularly children of the individual. This could prove some genealogical links and perhaps mention some children who do not appear in the Parish Registers. From the historical point of view, a good deal of social and economic history can be revealed, giving an idea of the social standing of your relative. You should be wary though, since because the eldest son inherited all of the land and buildings and did not receive any of the moveable property if his father died without a will, he may not be mentioned in the testament. Wills are the most likely source of details of your family's day-to-day life and therefore a very valuable source.

All Scottish testaments are stored in the National Archives of Scotland except for those from Orkney and Shetland, which are kept in the local archives. Before the Reformation, control over testaments was held by Church courts, but these were abolished and in 1564 commissary courts were established. Records survive for twenty-two commissary courts and one of their functions was to confirm testaments, with the Edinburgh Commissariot having authority throughout Scotland and for those who died abroad. This means you may need to check the Edinburgh court as well as the local court for the area in which your relative died.

In 1823 the sheriff courts took over responsibility for testamentary matters.

The Scottish Archive Network (SCAN) has prepared one consolidated index to all Scottish testaments up to 1901 which is now searchable on the Scottish Documents Web site. This can be searched by name, or other words included in the index, such as place or occupation. SCAN is also undertaking a massive digitization project to produce electronic versions of all the original testaments which, once completed, will be able to be viewed on computer screens as images linked to the index entries. This service will not be available on the Web, only in the National Archives of Scotland. However, high-quality copies can be ordered through the Web site. There are annual printed volumes indexing the testaments from 1876 to 1959, available in the National Archives of Scotland. If you do not have access to the Internet, there are various printed indexes to testaments, including one for each commissariot to 1800. For further details about the printed indexes, consult *Tracing Your Scottish Ancestors* (Sinclair 1997).

You may find it helpful to refer to *A Formulary of Old Scots Legal Documents* by Peter Gouldesborough (1985) which gives guidance on the standard format used in many Scots legal documents, including testaments and also the next two series of records to be described, retours and sasines.

RETOURS, OR SERVICES OF HEIRS

As we mentioned in the previous section, land or houses, or 'heritable property' as it is described, could not be left in a will until after 1868. Inheritance of this type of property was recorded in the retours, or services of heirs – either special retours, which named the property, or general retours, which did not. The other details to be found are the names of the heir and the relative whose property is being inherited, their relationship and possibly the date of death of the relative.

The retours begin in 1530 and were written in Latin until 1847, except for the years 1652 to 1659. It is important to search for a considerable period of time after the death of the earlier property owner because the retours were sometimes not recorded until well after the date of death. Although the originals are in the National Archives of Scotland, there are printed indexes which can be found in large reference libraries and these can sometimes provide sufficient detail, especially in a case when a son succeeded his father. The indexes have the added advantage of being in English. The index from 1425 to 1700 is arranged by county and gives references to two published volumes of summaries of the retours, which include most of the information. These summaries are also available in large reference libraries and a CD-ROM version has been published by the Scottish Genealogy Society. Details of the period covered by each volume of the printed 'Indexes to the Services of Heirs in Scotland' from 1700 onwards can be found on the National Archives of Scotland Web site.

SASINES

One of the most important series of records held in the National Archives of Scotland are the registers of sasines, which record the transfer of ownership of land and houses from 1617. This is a wonderful resource and there is no equivalent in England. If your family owned even a small piece of land or a small cottage, it should be possible to gather some details about them from the sasines. Quite often fathers granted land to their children and there could be a mention of previous grants with the chance of other relatives being named. Even if no family links are established in the transfer of the property concerned, there will be information about its location and boundaries (if land) and often the occupations of the two parties involved.

From 1617 to 1868 there was a General Register of Sasines, recording property in any area of Scotland, and various Particular Registers of Sasines recording property in a particular county. The period 1869 onwards is covered by a register for each county. As well as these, the royal burghs had their own registers, beginning at various dates. To make a comprehensive search for the earlier period you will need to check three registers if you think your family had property in a royal burgh; firstly the Burgh Register, secondly the Particular Register of Sasines for the area concerned and finally the General Register. If their property was outwith the royal burghs, the second and third of these will have to be consulted.

Although there are some indexes, not all areas and periods have been covered. Figure 7.1 is a brief summary of the indexes available.

Figure 7.1 A summary of the indexes of registers of sasines.

General Register	1617–1720 and 1781–1868
Particular Registers	1617–1780 some indexes, some of which have been published, and 1781–1868
Registers for each county	1869–
Burgh Registers	some indexed from 1809

The index from 1781 is arranged by county and covers both the General and Particular Registers, so this makes a search a little easier. It refers to the sasine abridgements which will probably give you all the information you require, but if you need to consult the full entries they are often in Latin. It is helpful to be familiar with the layout if you are likely to be looking at the full entries and Gouldesbrough's *Formulary of Old Scots Legal Documents* will give you guidance here. Both persons and places are indexed for 1781–1830 and 1872 onwards, but otherwise normally just the persons are indexed. The indexes of places for large towns in some cases list specific streets, but there are also entries such as 'Glasgow: Tenements in'.

The vast majority of the sasines are kept in the National Archives of Scotland, but some Burgh Registers are in local archives, namely the register for Glasgow and the registers for Aberdeen and Dundee before 1809. The Registers of Scotland, the organisation which now deals with the registration of land ownership, is based at Erskine House in Edinburgh, but there is also an office in Glasgow which stores the sasine abridgements for the 'counties' of Dunbarton, Glasgow and Renfrew. This may prove more convenient in some cases for researchers in the west of Scotland, but the drawback is that a charge is made for each person or property searched for.

Figure 7.2 is an example of an entry in the sasine abridgements for Fife.

Figure 7.2 Example of an entry in the sasine abridgements for Fife.

(1125)   May 10 1785.
DAVID DRYSDALE, Smith, Freuchie, and Jean Peattie, his spouse, Seised, in fee & liferent respectively, Apr. 28 1785 – in a Tenement in FREUCHIE, par. Falkland; – on Disp. by John Ramsay, Weaver, North Shields, to James Dryburgh, Merchant, Markinch, Dec. 31 1773; and Disp. & Assig. by him, Nov. 6 1784.
       P. R. 35. 205.

Sasines can sometimes be used to trace the history of a family and of land over several generations such as in the case of the Crawfurd family of Jordanhill, where there are sasines registered in 1698, 1679, 1657 and 1628 recording the transfer of the lands of Jordanhill to various members of the family.

REGISTERS OF DEEDS

These registers cover a wide variety of matters which involved some form of legal transaction. The most commonly recorded documents are bonds detailing loans of money while other deeds deal with settlements of testaments, marriage contracts, arrangements for apprenticeships and miscellaneous agreements between individuals. Finding a deed should fill in a little more detail of the life of the relative concerned and add some more colour to the picture you are building up.

Until 1809, deeds could be registered in any court, but from then on this function was restricted to the court of session, sheriff courts and royal burgh courts. As in the case of retours, deeds are sometimes not registered until years after the transaction had taken place. Figure 7.3 gives brief details of the various courts, the dates of the registers and whether they are indexed.

To make a thorough search, you will need to check the court of session registers and the registers for any other court covering the

Figure 7.3 Registers of deeds and their indexes.

Name of Court	Registers	Indexes
Court of session	From early 16th century	1554–95
		1705–7
		1714–15
		1750–2
		1765
		1770–present
Sheriff courts	Some from 16th century	Very few
	Some published	
Royal burgh courts	Some from 16th century	Very few
Commissary courts	Up to 1808	Peebles, 1755–62
Local courts	Up to 1747	None

area you are interested in. Most of these are in the National Archives of Scotland but there may be some in local archives. It is also worth mentioning that there are many deeds in the gifts and deposits collections in the national archives of scotland, but it may be rather difficult to trace a relevant deed, although see the section on the gifts and deposits collections later in this chapter.

KIRK SESSION RECORDS

These consist of the records of the body which ran the business of each Church of Scotland parish and since in the past this covered most aspects of people's lives, a great variety of information can be found there. The major items which usually appear are the organisation of relief for the poor of the parish and the disciplining of wrongdoers, with the individual's names being listed. Misconduct of parishioners might be 'breaking the Sabbath', by, perhaps, creating a disturbance when they should have been in church, or, the most commonly mentioned offence, fornication. Other matters could include lists of communicants or church members and details of the appointment of schoolmasters. These records are a major source for information on the ordinary people, containing the main listings of the poor to be found, but since they are not indexed it can be a laborious task to search them. The National Archives of Scotland has a fairly complete collection of Kirk session records but local archives sometimes have copies.

POOR RELIEF TO 1845

Up until the Poor Law Act of 1845, assistance to the poor was organised by the heritors (landowners) and the Kirk session of every parish. Sometimes separate lists were kept of payments to the poor of the parish, but more likely this information will be found mixed up with other business in the general records of the heritors and Kirk sessions. Again the main collection of these is held in the National Archives of Scotland with separate listings of heritors records and church records which include those of the Kirk sessions. In the burghs, although poor relief was dispensed, the records often give few details, but those for Edinburgh and Glasgow are rather more useful and can be found in the relevant local archive.

NONCONFORMIST RECORDS

Although in the past the vast majority of Scots were adherents of the Church of Scotland, there were many nonconformist churches whose records have survived in varying degrees of completeness and which tend to be scattered in various locations. From the eighteenth century up until the Disruption in 1843, there were various breakaways from the established Church of Scotland, with the Disruption, which resulted in the formation of the Free Church of Scotland, being the most important. After this, mergers of denominations began to take place and by 1929 many of these Churches had reunited with the Church of Scotland. Many of the records of these Churches are kept in the National Archives of Scotland and include baptisms, marriages and burials, lists of communicants and minute books. Two of the main Churches represented are the Free Church of Scotland and the United Presbyterian Church of Scotland.

As far as the records of the Roman Catholic Church are concerned, the National Archives of Scotland have photocopies of all pre-1855 registers of baptisms, marriages and deaths, which could ease the searcher's task considerably. One register dates back to 1703, but in general they begin in the nineteenth century. The parish priests hold either the originals or copies of their own registers, while the archives of the Archdiocese of Glasgow also have registers for some of the parishes in Glasgow and the surrounding area.

Again, in the case of the Episcopal Church of Scotland, most of the records are still held by the local clergy, with a few originals and microfilm copies in the National Archives for Scotland. You should find the surveys of the National Register of Archives for Scotland helpful here, since all known Episcopal Church records have been surveyed and lists produced. The National Register of Archives for Scotland is discussed later in this chapter

Finally, there are the Baptist, Congregational, Methodist, Quaker and Unitarian Churches. Some of these records are stored in the National Archives of Scotland while Glasgow City Archives has a sizeable collection of nonconformist records for almost all of these Churches apart from the Catholic Church. As you would expect, these cover Glasgow and surrounding areas, but the Congregational Church records come from all parts of Scotland. For the Baptist Church, the individual church should be contacted. For nonconformist records in general it is worth checking the National Register of Archives for Scotland for possible locations, or the headquarters of the Church concerned.

VALUATION ROLLS BEFORE 1855

Some rolls exist in the National Archives of Scotland for this earlier period, but they are isolated and sometimes they list the value of the lands but not the names of the proprietors and occupiers. The earliest of these date from 1643, while some have been published. You may find useful *A Directory of Land Ownership in Scotland c. 1770* by Loretta R. Timperley (1976), which takes its information mainly from valuation rolls. The early nineteenth century is better provided for, but, as in the case of the earlier period, in the royal burghs the tax was usually paid in one lump sum and those paying were not normally listed.

If you do find family members mentioned in valuation rolls, you will probably only succeed in locating them at a particular place at a particular date since the information will be very brief and is more likely to mention proprietors than occupiers. This information might, however, provide a basis for tracing them in the registers of sasines which would give much fuller details.

For more detailed information on what is available for valuation rolls in the National Archives of Scotland, consult Sinclair's *Tracing Your Scottish Ancestors.*

HEARTH TAX AND POLL TAX

These two taxes were introduced for fairly short periods in the 1690s, the hearth tax from 1691 to 1695 and the poll tax from 1693 to 1699, and although this is a fairly serious limitation, they do provide listings of a considerable proportion of the population. All landowners and tenants were liable to pay for the number of hearths in their houses, while the poll tax was levied on all adults who did not depend on charity. Unfortunately the records are not complete and in the case of the hearth tax some list the amount collected but not individuals' names. The arrangement of the records is by county and then by parish, with the poll tax having two series of records which both need to be checked. If you do find your family mentioned in the poll tax records, children's names may also be included.

The original documents are in the National Archives of Scotland, but there are some published lists.

TRADES

As you can imagine, those involved in trade tended to be concentrated in the royal burghs, where such matters were well regulated. In order to be allowed to practise a trade in the royal burghs, an individual was required to be admitted as a burgess. Some lists of burgesses have been published by the Scottish Record Society, in particular those for Edinburgh (1406–1841) and Glasgow (1573–1846). Otherwise, admissions can be found in burgh records, some in the National Archives of Scotland but many in local archives. Since newly admitted burgesses were often sons or sons-in-law of burgesses, this relationship is mentioned in the records.

There also existed, in the burghs, influential craft guilds or incorporations which kept records of members and here again they were often sons or sons-in-law of members, or were apprenticed to a member of the craft. Published lists exist in some cases and the original records can be found in local archives, the National Archives of Scotland or listed in the National Register of Archives for Scotland surveys.

Because of the large proportion of burgesses and craft members who were admitted by right of their relationship to an existing member, it is possible to trace back several generations through these records, which can thus prove a very fruitful source.

John Brock was admitted as a Glasgow Burgess in 1787 as eldest son of William Brock, weaver. Checking back, we find that William had been admitted in 1776 as the eldest son of another William Brock, weaver. This William, the grandfather of John, appears in 1743 and was the eldest son of Robert Brock, deceased, gardener, who was admitted in 1719 as married to Agnes, daughter of the deceased John

Duncan, gardener. We could then continue our search by following up the Duncan family. You can see the usefulness of this source, which, in this example, took us back four generations in only a few minutes of research.

The apprenticeship system was widespread until relatively recently and normally the father of the new apprentice entered into an agreement, called an indenture, with the master to whom he was apprenticed. These are mentioned in the records of the craft concerned, but not many of the indentures themselves have survived. Some appear in the registers of deeds and there is a collection of Edinburgh indentures for 1613–1783 in the National Archives of Scotland. A published list of Edinburgh apprentices (1583–1755) is also available. As a result of the imposition of stamp duty on indentures in 1710, there are records of Scottish apprentices for 1710–1811 in the Public Record Office in London.

Unfortunately, if your relatives were tradesmen beyond the burghs, there are unlikely to be any records available. The only sources for them are few and far between, being the records of mutual benefit societies such as the Society of Free Fishermen of Newhaven. The main repository for these is the National Archives of Scotland.

Anyone selling alcoholic drink had, from 1756, to be licensed and this covered the burghs and the counties. The granting of these licences was carried out by the burgh court or the Justices of the Peace for the county and their records are kept in the National Archives of Scotland or local archives, beginning mainly in the nineteenth century.

MERCHANT SEAMEN

Although difficult to search without fairly precise details of the ship or port concerned, there are vouchers of payments of bounties for whaling (1750–1825) and for herring fishing (1752–96). These vouchers named the crews and are available in the National Archives of Scotland.

INDEX OF BIRTHS, MARRIAGES AND DEATHS

Another source which should be mentioned is the *Scots Magazine*, which published notices of births, marriages and deaths of the more affluent sections of society. An index to these is kept in the Office of the Lord Lyon in Edinburgh for 1739–1826.

GIFTS AND DEPOSITS COLLECTIONS

This title covers a very wide range of documents which have been gifted or lent to the National Archives of Scotland by individuals, families, businesses and organisations. These documents may provide you with useful information, particularly if your family lived on a large estate. If the estate papers are amongst the gifts and deposits collections, your family's name may well be mentioned. The online catalogue of the National Archives of Scotland allows the searcher to look for any word or name which appears in the entry for each document in a collection. The entries include a brief description of the contents of the document and so often names can be mentioned, especially in the case of correspondence. A useful category of material found in the gifts and deposits collections are wages books, although the contents are not indexed.

NATIONAL REGISTER OF ARCHIVES FOR SCOTLAND (NRAS)

You will have gathered by now that once you move beyond the three main categories of records held in New Register House, the Civil Registers, census records and Old Parish Registers, most archival material is scattered in various locations. Although there is never likely to be a complete listing of all collections and their whereabouts, the National Register of Archives for Scotland, or NRAS, is an attempt to provide one. Since its foundation in 1946, it has gathered information on and conducted surveys of archive collections held outwith the National Archives of Scotland by individuals, businesses and organisations, including local authority archives. Their lists of surveys range from the very small to the very large, for example from the one-page survey of the records of The Royal High School Athletic Club, Edinburgh Rugby Section, to the 144-page survey of the Scottish Episcopal Church Congregations in the Diocese of Edinburgh, or large estate collections such as those of the Dukes of Hamilton, Argyll and Roxburghe.

The NRAS is administered by the National Archives of Scotland, based in its West Register House site in Charlotte Square, Edinburgh, and the index to the surveys can be consulted in the National Archives of Scotland, National Library of Scotland, many of the older university libraries and local authority archives. Any types of record can be listed and so if you have been unsuccessful in tracing a particular source in the obvious locations it is worthwhile checking the NRAS. For a possible way of searching this through the Internet see Chapter 5.

MAKING USE OF THE SOURCES

So these are the sources, or at least the main ones, but how can you make use of what you find? The historical information giving details about the lives of your family and the environment in which they lived can be very interesting but we would hope that you will incorporate it into some form of narrative family history. We will describe some means of going about this in the next chapter. Before moving on to this stage, we should consider how to extend the framework of your family tree using the genealogical information you have gleaned from the sources described in Chapters 6 and 7.

The most important facts needed to make genealogical links are name, date and place of birth or baptism, marriage, and death or burial. If these are known, you will have a good chance of tracing a record of the event. This in turn may either make a genealogical link, with the parents' names given in a baptismal record or perhaps a father's name in a marriage entry, or give enough data to lead you back to an earlier event which can then establish a link. A record of burial giving the person's age may in some cases help you find the baptism, although you will probably need extra evidence to confirm this.

When tracing your family in the earlier period we have been looking at, you will very often find that only one of these important facts is known, this being the name. Everything else has to be sought out by deduction and by building up a body of evidence, similar to that in a legal case, in order to prove that each record that you find really does refer to the individual you are tracing and not to someone else of the same name.

In the case of working back from a marriage to a baptism, you will usually need to estimate the age of the bride and groom, since it is unlikely to be given. Then you can search for baptisms in the period calculated according to their estimated ages. This could range from 16 to perhaps 40, but is probably on average likely to be between 20 and 25, although average age at marriage has varied at different times in history and can also be affected by local conditions. You may have found one or both of the fathers' names in the marriage entry, which will be a big help in correctly identifying the baptism you are seeking.

The other factor – place – could also prove to be a problem. The marriage entry might state the parishes of the bride and groom but if it does not it is probable that the marriage took place in the bride's parish. All you can do, without evidence to the contrary, is deduce that the parish listed for each at their marriage was the one in which they were baptised. This, of course, may not be the case and when no parishes are named, the task becomes more difficult, especially in the case of the groom.

In making the connection between a baptism and the marriage of the parents, things may be a little easier. The registers can be searched for possible older brothers and sisters and then the marriage, but you may find neither these nor a marriage, since the family could have moved from another parish where the marriage and other baptisms were registered. Another possibility, if baptisms are found but no marriage, is that the parish that you are searching in was the husband's parish but the marriage took place in the wife's parish.

Although in the past movement was less common than today, especially over long distances, there was often movement in and out of parishes within a ten-mile radius, so if you lose trace of a family you could try the few surrounding parishes.

One other consideration which may assist you is the traditional naming pattern often followed in Scotland. Further details can be found in the section on Christian names in Chapter 9.

We have outlined here some of the difficulties you may encounter. You must be satisfied that you have made correct identifications for all those included in your family history. This is an area particularly studied by historical demographers in their work on nominal record linkage and its use in family reconstitution. If you want to follow up this important method of establishing reliable genealogical links, you should consult *Identifying People in the Past*, edited by E. A. Wrigley (1973). Genealogists have always been used to making such links, but the historical demographers, looking at large numbers of families and making use of computers in their work, have formalised the methods. It is obviously important to make the correct links and we hope that this section has emphasised this and given you some clues on how to tackle this aspect of family history.

CHAPTER 8

PRESENTING YOUR FAMILY HISTORY

As a hunter-gatherer in the field of family history you will probably amass quite a quantity of facts. Names, dates, occupations and other snippets of information will abound, but if you have followed our advice earlier in the book, these details should be well organised and easily accessible. What will almost certainly be lacking in your collection of family history materials is narrative. Perhaps you may have stories or reminiscences gathered from elderly relatives and written down or recorded on audio cassette. The collection could also include obituaries or newspaper reports about members of your family. However, this sort of material is not likely to occur often and when it does forms an isolated example of narrative. This chapter is about producing some form of continuous narrative history of your family in which you put flesh on the bones of the skeleton family tree you have constructed. In doing this, you will be able to bring together the fruits of your labours and present them in a readable form which hopefully will prove to be not only a source of satisfaction to yourself but also of interest to relatives and perhaps even a wider audience.

WHEN SHOULD THIS BE DONE?

Obviously a reasonable amount of information is required before making a start, but to put off too long is not advisable. You may have relatives who have helped you out with facts which they can remember and documents which they own and who would be keen to see the results of your investigations. It is probably unlikely that you will complete your researches for a considerable time, if ever, so do not wait for that moment, particularly considering the fact that word processing facilities are now widely available. This makes it very easy for you to begin constructing your narrative history in the knowledge that if you discover new information it can easily be incorporated and printed out without the need for retyping whole sections or pages. Our advice would be to compose a basic narrative as soon as possible and update it regularly. When you decide it is full enough and in a presentable form, it can be printed out and reproduced for wider circulation.

A NARRATIVE HISTORY?

The simplest form of written history which you might consider using is a family tree in chart form along with associated notes on the various individuals. The names on the chart, or charts, are numbered and then on separate pages fuller details can be given for each numbered individual. These notes could range from the dates and places of birth, baptism, marriage, death and burial to extensive biographies, depending on the information you have and what you feel is appropriate.

However, we will look here at writing a narrative family history which uses family tree charts to aid clarity while the narrative itself forms the basis.

The first main type of narrative is that found in *Burke's Peerage* and *Burke's Landed Gentry*, and in genealogy software packages. These use indentation on the page, along with various sequences of numbers and letters, to indicate different generations. The information about each individual tends to be relatively brief in this form of history.

If you are interested in using this format, have a look at some examples in Burke's publications mentioned above, which will provide a good guide as to how this method works.

James Balfour Paul wrote an introduction to Margaret Stuart's *Scottish Family History* published in 1930, in which he describes various approaches to writing a family history. The **anecdotal method** is usually quite easy to read, being chatty and amusing. It does not normally include many references to sources of information and does not quote from these sources to any great extent. The **historical method** attempts to place the family in its historical context, looking at how historical events affected the family and, perhaps, what impact the family made on history. The most comprehensive approach he calls the **scientific method** in which all the available facts are recorded, full references to sources are provided and sources are quoted at length, possibly in a second volume containing only extracts from source materials.

You will have to make your own decision about which approach or combination of approaches you wish to take, but we would certainly hope that you would include an element of the historical method in whatever you decide upon. No family exists in a vacuum and knowledge of the community and environment in which it lives is vitally important in reaching a proper understanding of its history. By placing the family in historical context, you can pick out features which your family had in common with its surrounding community and also those features which were different. This type of approach may also help your family history appeal to local historians and others who may then be able to draw on your work to assist them with their own endeavours on a larger scale. Whatever methods you employ to write up your family history, there are a number of important points to be considered.

- You may need to decide whether to impose censorship on the material to be included in your history. Perhaps this will depend on who is likely to be reading the end product, but it could be that certain stories or facts gathered in the course of your researches would cause offence, so it is something worth thinking about.
- It is helpful to have clear in your mind a procedure for describing the history of the various branches of your family, since without a clear structure the history could become very confusing to everyone but yourself. The best plan is to begin with the earliest known ancestor, giving their story, including information about their spouse or spouses and children as they appear in the course of their life. After giving their date of death, repeat the names of his wife and children and also give brief details about any of them who will not be described more fully later. For those to be mentioned again within the text, it is useful to quote after their names the pages referring to them. In most cases it is probably best to complete one line of descent down to the most recent family members as one chapter and then consider other branches in later sections of the history.
- There are a number of features which you can use to improve the clarity and add to the interest of your account. Most important here are **family tree charts**. For a large and complicated family history you might need a main chart supplemented by others for each branch of the family. Only very brief details will be required on the charts since the individuals will be fully described in the text, but you may want to indicate the page numbers of the individuals' entries against their names on the chart.
- An **index** and **table of contents** are also very worthwhile if the

finished work is of reasonable length. Be careful to make it very clear in the index which particular person is being referred to, since so often there will be several family members with the same name. You could use dates, places of residence and occupations to distinguish between them.

- **References** to your sources of information should be included to either a lesser or greater extent depending on your viewpoint. To avoid interrupting the flow of your narrative, use numbers in the text, with the corresponding notes appearing at the foot of the page or at the end of either the chapter or the whole work.

- **Illustrations** will obviously increase the interest of your work and so if possible you should include pictures of members of the family, of places where they lived, were educated and worked, churches where they were baptised and married, tombstones, medals and perhaps even coats of arms.

- Although your researches will have gathered plenty of information about the members of your family, for the purposes of a family history, particularly one using the historical method, you will need to build up some background information on the national and local history of the time. This should include not only events but also the social and economic conditions that would affect your family. You could use a chronology such as Steinberg's *Historical Tables* (1991) to identify events of national importance. Otherwise, consult national and local histories, social and economic histories and, where appropriate, histories of occupations and institutions with which family members were associated, such as churches, schools and universities. The best place to seek advice on what sources are available is the local history or local studies section of the libary for the area you are interested in. Particularly important sources for local history are the three series of statistical accounts of Scotland, with a section devoted to each parish in Scotland. The 'old' statistical account, published 1791–9 and the new statistical account of 1845 have entries written by the parish ministers and vary greatly in length, depending on the interests of each minister. The third statistical account, 1951–92, was written by a variety of contributors regarded as being knowledgeable about specific areas, but is probably, at present, of less value to family historians than the two earlier accounts. The relevant sections should certainly be regarded as essential reading for anyone writing a family history. The first two accounts are now on the Web, making them much more accessible to the general public. It is worthwhile putting some effort into this background research as this should help you to produce a much better end product. It will allow you to produce a real history of your family in historical context as opposed to a mere chronicle of family events.

Examples of narrative family histories

A reasonable strategy would be to focus on a significant ancestor. The definition of 'significant' will vary from one person's family history to another's. However, a basic definition would seem to be someone about whom you have quite a bit of detail, both in strict genealogical terms and perhaps also in terms of their work or special interests.

One approach would be to look at an ancestor and write up about that ancestor, his parents, siblings, spouse and children. The narrative, as mentioned previously, will probably be a 'work in progress' rather than a completed work. The example given in figure 8.1 is written for a family readership, rather than for a wider audience.

Another possible approach could be to write up one aspect of an ancestor's life and work, as shown in figure 8.2.

WEB PAGES

With the relatively widespread use of the World Wide Web, a new format for presenting family history material has become available to the family historian. It has brought the possibility of personal publishing (on the Web) to a far wider public than ever before. In theory, virtually all types of material can be published on the Web: text; family trees of various sorts, both textual and graphical; other graphics, including photographs and documents; sound; and video. In practice, not all of these formats are straightforward to deal with, but there is still plenty of scope for the non-specialist.

There are different ways in which you can prepare Web pages. Most pages are written in HTML (Hypertext Markup Language) so you could begin by learning the basic elements of HTML and writing your own Web pages from scratch. Otherwise (or in addition) you could use either a genealogy package, most of which now have the facility to create Web pages, or a Web editing or authoring package, the best of these at the time of writing being probably Dreamweaver, produced by Macromedia, and FrontPage, produced by Microsoft. The cost implications may be important, with the financial investment in the first option being virtually zero, except perhaps to purchase one or two good books on HTML, but the

Figure 8.1 Example of a narrative family history: an ancestor and his family.

Henry Thomas Winch (1849–1899)

HENRY THOMAS WINCH was born on **11 March 1849** in Queenborough, Kent. He was **baptised on 17 April 1849** by William Worth, a Wesleyan minister.

WHO WERE HIS PARENTS?

His father was **JAMES HENRY WINCH**, a fisherman, and his mother was **ELIZABETH WINCH (née UNDERDOWN)**.

James Henry Winch and Elizabeth Underdown were married on 1 January 1844 in the parish church of Frindsbury in Kent. James Edward was the son of **EDWARD** (mariner) and **AMY WINCH**. Elizabeth Underdown was the daughter of **THOMAS UNDERDOWN** (mariner).

The witnesses to the marriage were named as Stephen and Sarah Underdown.

From the 1851 census for 127 South Street, Queenborough, Elizabeth Winch (ms Underdown) was born in Upnor, about 1820–1.

From the 1861 census, the family lived at 115 High Street.

From the 1871 census for 99 High Street, Elizabeth Winch's occupation is given as 'Linen Draper Shop Keeper'.

From the 1881 census for 99 High Street, Elizabeth Winch (ms Underdown) is, by that time, a widow and her occupation listed as 'Nurse'.

WHO WERE HIS SIBLINGS?

Henry Thomas had four sisters, **AGNES** (born in 1846–7), **ELIZABETH FANNY** (born 27 February 1852), **HARRIET LOUISA** (born 11 May 1854), **JOSEPHINE AMY** (born 13 April 1857), and a younger brother **JAMES EDWARD** (born 4 September 1860).

AGNES is only to be found so far (aged 4) in the 1851 census for 127 South Street, Queenborough – as the daughter of James Winch (fisherman – aged 39) and Elizabeth Winch (aged 30), and the elder sister of Henry Winch (aged 2). She does not appear in later censuses, and no further details are known by the family.

ELIZABETH FANNY did not marry. She was 'in service' for most of her working life. She became blind in old age and went to live with William Henry Winch (one of the sons of James Edward) and his family in 1937. Betty Cummings (ms Winch) has one or two of her personal effects, including a wooden deed box, dated 1879. Elizabeth Fanny Winch died on 5 September 1941.

HARRIET LOUISA was an 'immoveable invalid' (1881 census) and in later life was a lacemaker, living part of the year in Queenborough with one of James Edward's sons, Sid and his wife Winnie, in order to qualify for poor relief; for the rest of the year she lived in Maidstone with her brother James Edward. It is also said that she lived in a tiny cottage in Queenborough, where she did her intricate lacework by the light of a tiny oil lamp.

Figure 8.2 Example of a narrative family history: an ancestor's life and work.

The Spritsail Barge Career of Henry Thomas Winch (1849–1899)

[ADD PHOTOGRAPH HERE]

HENRY THOMAS WINCH and family lived in Queenborough, according to the 1881 census with his parents at 99 High Street, and, according to the 1891 census, at 85 High Street.

As family lore would have it, he is reputed to have had the 'freedom of the Port of London'.

Perhaps this extract from the Register of Contracts of the Watermen & Lightermen's Company throws some light on this:

Lower Thames Street EC
Winch Harry Keep articled Henry Thomas Winch for 2 years
– commencing 9 February 1897

Normally you had to be between 14 and 20 to be bound to a Freeman of the Company and serve a five-, six- or seven year apprenticeship. Men too old to serve the apprenticeship – (Henry Thomas Winch was 47) – could serve a two-year 'contract' to a Master Waterman or Lighterman, and thereby be admitted to the 'freedom of the Company'. From the records it would appear that Henry Thomas died before completing his two-year period of being articled.

Another piece of lore was that he was master of a spritsail barge which carried china clay between Sheerness in Kent and Newhaven in Scotland. It is possible that this could have been the chalky sediment of the River Medway (known locally as the 'Mudway'), dredged to keep the channels clear and used in cement manufacture. A further possibility is that one cargo could have been shale products from the Firth of Forth area (e.g. Polkemmet), shipped from Leith. This may give a reason for being in Newhaven, Scotland in 1877, where he met his wife.

From the sole surviving family barge photograph (probably taken in the late 1880s or early 1890s), the barge pictured is a tank barge, has no davits, has capstan winches, three part vang falls, and would seem to be of about sixteen or seventeen feet beam; from its size, it would appear to have been suitable only for plying the estuarial waters of the Swale, Medway and Thames.

[ADD PHOTOGRAPH HERE]

Henry Thomas Winch, at the helm, with family,
on the River Swale, off Queenborough

At one time, the writer thought that this barge, because of its links with Queenborough, could have been the barge *Rosa* (reg. no. 78525), of thirty-six tons, built by Josiah Bird at Conyer in 1878, registered at Faversham, owned originally by F. Bunting of 34 Cyprus Road, Faversham, and which later passed into the hands of the Sheppey Glue Works at Queenborough.

According to R. H. Perks of the Society for Spritsail Barge Research:
From the Register of F. W. Monger, Inspector of nuisances at Faversham 1881–2, barges found at Faversham: *Who'd a Thout It* spritsail, built Limehouse 1825, thirty-five tons. Master Captain Winch. The barge was owned by Charles Hartnell of Limehouse, and was probably in the rubbish trade at the time of her arrival in Faversham.

East Kent Gazette – 15/1/1877. Reported the drowning of Captain James Winch of sailing barge *Alice Lloyd* of Rochester, owned by John Charles Laurence of Queenborough (who became bankrupt in June 1904). While coming back on board late at night Captain Winch jumped off the pier into his barge boat, fell overboard and was drowned. Could this be some relation? Henry Lawrence of Queenborough owned the spl *Brilliant* in 1881.

investment in time learning the language being more significant. You may already be using a genealogy package for storing and organising your information, so it might be a good option to use this to create your Web pages, but you will find that you are restricted by the pre-determined format of some pages. It all depends on what you want as your end product. Software such as Dreamweaver and FrontPage is fairly costly, although there is a cut-down version of FrontPage, called FrontPage Express, included as part of Windows 98 and upwards and also as part of Microsoft Office 2000 Developer. The advantage of these packages is their greater sophistication and flexibility and also their ability to organise and keep control of large Web sites. They are recommended if you have an elaborate Web site in mind. Although Web authoring packages are useful and powerful tools, it is still beneficial to have a knowledge of HTML in order to understand the workings of the software, particularly if you wish to create more advanced Web pages. The software may produce a result which was not quite what you intended and a knowledge of HTML can help you to make the necessary adjustments.

Taking all of these factors into account, our advice for the average family historian would be to use your genealogy package to create Web pages, but for others who require something slightly different, consider the other possibilities we have outlined.

Genealogy packages will produce family charts as Web pages in many formats and for examples of these you could look at the Web sites describing some of these packages, listed in the software section of Cyndi's List. Drop line charts are not so commonly found on the Web although this form of graphical display of a family tree is generally the most comprehensive and easily understood means of showing family relationships. It is possible, with a bit of effort, to draw this type of family tree using a program such as the 'Draw' feature of Microsoft Word. Once the tree is completed in Word, it can then be copied and pasted into a graphics program, such as Adobe Photoshop, where it is saved for use on a Web page. It becomes more of a problem if the tree is larger than A4 size, but with some extra tinkering a good result can be achieved. An additional feature can be added by making these image maps, which allow users to click on a name on the tree which will take them to another page, with text or a picture, or both, relating to that individual.

As far as text, photographs, documents, sound and video are concerned, these can all be accommodated on a Web site and can also be produced by genealogy packages. If the results you achieve with your geneaology package do not suit your needs and you wish to create

Web pages independently, you should consult the suggested reading material listed in the Bibliography.

CASE STUDY ON USING THE WEB

For a fairly straightforward example of how you could present information on Web pages, have a look at the Timperley of Hintlesham Web site. This has a homepage with some basic information about some of the earlier members of the family and a number of external links. One link is to another site, based in the USA, devoted to any family with the surname Timperley, others are to a site about the present-day Hintlesham Hall, which is a hotel, including pictures of the house, and one to the Boughton House site. This stately home was once owned by Sir Edward Montagu, an ancestor of some of the Timperleys. You will see that some use of graphics has been made on this page. The major part of the site consists of a number of pages giving details of descendants of the family. These are displayed in the format found in *Burke's Peerage* and now also in many reports and Web pages produced by genealogy packages, using indentation to distinguish different generations. In this case they have been created from scratch in HTML format, rather than by using a genealogy package. This means there is greater control over how the end result looks. Very often in these types of family chart the data is displayed in one continuous sequence, using numbers and/or letters as well as indentation to help identify the various generations. This can sometimes be difficult to follow, particularly for an inexperienced reader, but the facility to link pages, which is such a basic feature of the Web, is ideal for improving the clarity of these charts. As you can see from this example, usually only three generations appear on one page. If the individuals in the second generation had many children or if there are descendants in the next generation to be shown, then a link to another page has been made to continue the line further. Using this method, it is unnecessary to use numbers or letters for different generations since such a small number of generations are displayed on one page. For example, one of the pages shows three children of John Timperley Hicks, the children of these three and some of the next generation, where no further descendants are known. Because John Barnard Hicks, a grandson of John Timperley Hicks, had many children and later descendants are known, there is a link to a new page to show his descendants.

The site could be developed to include links to brief biographies of individuals, since only the basic facts are included at present.

There is a page entitled Research which describes some specific areas of research that has been done on the connected families and other pages feature two graphical family trees using drop line charts. These employ the methods we have described earlier in this chapter and the Timperley family tree is also an 'image map' with live links from names to pages with further information about the individuals. A larger example of a graphical family tree is the Crawfurd of Jordanhill family tree (see list of Web sites).

Other features of the Timperley site include, a page incorporating a small response form intended for those descended from the family to send in by e-mail. Secondly, there is a search page from which simple searches can be made of the site. This facility is provided free by a Web site search service. Finally, there is a Web counter which registers the number of hits on the site and gives some further information such as whether a search engine was used and what the search terms were. Again this is a free service with which you can register a non-commercial site.

As you can imagine, this site could be developed to include more external links and to use more graphics, but it should serve to illustrate a number of ways in which the Web can be used for this type of information.

OTHER FORMATS

Since today it is easy to make use of various media, you might want to try your hand at using audio cassette recordings, cassette and slide presentations, multimedia presentations, or video recordings to give your family history an added dimension. Perhaps you have already used audio cassettes to record relatives' reminiscences and some local libraries keep collections of oral history recorded in this format. Extracts could be used to make up a cassette to accompany the text of your history, the audio equivalent of a second volume containing extracts from sources, as mentioned earlier.

Cassette and slide presentations and video recordings could be used as an additional feature of a family history or, with a lot of planning, the whole work might be produced in one of these formats. Another possibility for presenting your family history to an audience is by means of presentation software such as Microsoft PowerPoint, which is available both for PC and Macintosh. This software would allow you to produce and show a kind of automated slide show, but in addition would permit you to incorporate text, sound, graphics and video material. The possibilities of such a presentation are really quite impressive – you could incorporate such material as portraits or photographs of ancestors, sections of charts or trees, recordings of voices recalling events within your family history, music, video clips of people and events which have relevance to your own family history and so on. Obviously there is scope here ranging from a fairly basic presentation to a very ambitious production, depending on your talents in this field. You may well not feel the need or inclination to venture into any media other than the written word, but we mention these as possibilities which not long ago would have been impracticable.

CHAPTER 9

FAMILY HERITAGE

WHAT'S IN A NAME?

Names, both Christian names and surnames, can range from the very common to the very unusual. An unusual name or combination of names can make a tremendous difference in the ability to identify the individual you are seeking. In city parishes with large numbers of baptisms, marriages and burials, there may be a number of persons of the same name registered round about the same date, given that the name is a fairly common one. On the other hand, if you are searching for an unusual name, there is a much greater chance of a correct identification. Customs for choosing Christian names, particularly in Scotland, can also lend a helping hand to the researcher. You may find some background information on names useful and interesting.

Originally people had only one name and surnames were adopted gradually, becoming established during the twelfth century. There are four main types of surname: local names, relationship names, occupational names and nicknames.

The local names could refer to a place of origin, such as de Bruce, originally from Brius (now Brix) in Normandy, or a residence such as Wood or Marsh. Nobles and great landowners who took their names from their lands were the first to have fixed surnames.

Relationship names tend to be patronymics, giving the name of the father, such as Williamson or Robertson. Since Mac means son of, all the names beginning with Mac are of this type, as are surnames of Irish origin beginning with O', such as O'Brien. At one time the patronymic changed with each generation but eventually many became established as fixed surnames. In the case of the Scottish clans, the names beginning with Mac often refer to the individual regarded as the founder of the clan.

This type of name often still changed from generation to generation in the Highlands well into the eighteenth century and in

Shetland into the nineteenth century. A number of variations in patronymics can be found. Sometimes the 'son' ending was dropped, leaving the Christian name of the ancestor as the surname. Another variation was the shortening of the name's ending to 's', Adams, Edwards, for example.

Occupational names include Smith, Baker and Butcher while nicknames could, among other things, refer to appearance or qualities. Amongst these surnames are White, Long, Good and Savage. There is some doubt about how many surnames which are apparently nicknames are in fact true nicknames. It may well be that many have other derivations which are difficult to discover.

CHANGES OF NAME

Although you probably assume that your own surname has remained the same for many generations, this may not be the case since there are various reasons why surnames may have changed. This could obviously pose problems for the family historian, so you should be aware of the possibilities.

In the Highlands especially, when the clan system was in operation it was common for individuals to take the surname of a powerful local clan whom they wished to support and whose protection they sought. This meant that many clansmen with names such as Campbell or Macdonald were not related to the chief they followed but regarded themselves as part of that clan.

Another reason for changes of names was due to the fact that a sizeable proportion of the Scottish population were of Gaelic or Irish origin, often with surnames which were unfamiliar or difficult to pronounce, and these were changed to what seemed like the nearest equivalent English name. As an example, we sometimes find the Gaelic name MacDhomhnaill becoming MacDonald and the Irish name Kearney becoming Cairnie.

Corruption of names can also come about, perhaps as a result of illiteracy and local accents. An example of this is the change from some of those named Timperley to Templey, which took place during the nineteenth century.

Finally, there is the possibility that someone adopted a different surname. This might be the name of an important patron, such as Thomas Cromwell, Henry VIII's Chancellor. His nephew Richard Williams became Richard Cromwell, a direct ancestor of Oliver Cromwell. In succeeding to property, often through an heiress, the inheritor might take the name of the family whose property they were inheriting. This might actually be a condition of the inheritance. Daniel Kerr of Kersland, living in the late sixteenth century, was the eldest son of Thomas Crawfurd of Jordanhill and Janet Kerr, but took his mother's name, as she was the heiress of Robert Kerr of Kersland.

CHRISTIAN NAMES

As far as Christian names are concerned, you may find some assistance from the traditional naming pattern often followed in Scotland. The eldest son was named after the father's father, the second son after the mother's father and the third son after the father. Daughters were named after first the mother's mother, then the father's mother and thirdly the mother. This can be used as a basis to work from, but should not be relied upon and would need confirmation from another source. This could sometimes lead to duplication of names, particularly in earlier times when the custom was more rigidly adhered to than in more recent times. Another reason for the duplication of Christian names was the desire to ensure that a particular name survived in the next generation. As a result, if a child was in very poor health, another might be given the same name, although both might eventually develop into healthy adults.

Other sources of Christian names might be from friends or events, for example Victoria at the time of the Queen's coronation. Foundlings were often given the name of the place they were found or the name of a sponsor, minister or elder at the baptism. It should also be mentioned that middle names were unusual until about 1830.

Pet names and different forms of name could prove significant in tracking down elusive relatives, some examples being Alexander/ Alastair; Agnes/Nancy; John/Ian; Jane/Jean; while Fred and Freddy could be short for either Alfred or Frederick.

THE SCOTTISH CLAN SYSTEM

Whatever their ancient origins, Celtic, Norse or Norman-French, by the thirteenth century the clan system was well established in the Highlands of Scotland. It was a distinct Gaelic tribal culture which, in its fifteenth century heyday, threatened the authority of the Stewart monarchs. Though increasingly brought into contact with the rest of Scotland, the clan system survived until its eventual dismantling, partly as a consequence of the final Jacobite uprising which ended at Culloden in 1746.

THE CLANS – THEIR HEYDAY AND
THEIR DEMISE

The clan system was part of a Gaelic tribal culture, completely separated by language, custom and geography from the 'Sassenach' or southerner (that is, of 'Saxon' origin – a word applicable both to the English and Lowland Scots). In Gaelic, the word *clann* means family or children. The clans lived off the land more or less self-sufficiently, with cattle as their main wealth. Stealing cattle (sometimes in order to survive) was widespread, as were territorial disputes between clans. The clansmen did not own land, only the chief, sometimes directly from the crown, sometimes from other superior clan chiefs. The most powerful chiefs in some places kept expensive courts and retainers for prestige and had virtual autonomy over matters of law and order within their territory. Not all of a clan chieftain's preoccupations were war-like. An important member of the chief's retinue was the bard, who could both compose an epic poem, perhaps recalling a feat of heroism in battle, and recite lineage, which was part of his role as the recorder of the clan's story. The clan piper was another hereditary post, of whom the MacCrimmons, hereditary pipers to the MacLeods, were the most famous. However, by the eighteenth century, with agricultural improvements spreading from the Lowlands and with some road-building taking place which made communications easier, clans and their chiefs were brought more and more into contact with 'southern' ways. Thus, even without the shock of Culloden and the violent reaction of the Lowland authorities (the banning of tartan, the forfeiting of estates and so on) the old clan system was gradually being absorbed into a modern economic society. This process of change was noted by Sir Walter Scott in his novel *Rob Roy*, where Rob can be seen as a symbol of the old, self-sufficient ways, which contrasted with his distant cousin, Bailie Nicol Jarvie, a Glasgow merchant preoccupied with progress and business. Even so, Rob also acts as a Jacobite agent and sympathiser (as did the real life Rob Roy), demonstrating that, inevitably, the clan system was a part of Scottish politics.

THE ORIGINS OF THE CLANS

Some clans have Norman roots and married into Celtic society: Cummings (Comyns); Hays (de la Haye); Frasers (La Frezeliäre – ultimately linked to the French *la fraise*, referring to the strawberry-shaped device on the family crest); Sinclair (St Clair); and Bruce

(Brix, a Normandy place name). Following early Viking raids on Scotland, others have Norse connections: the MacLeods of Skye are said to descend from Liot, son of a Norse king; the MacDougalls of Lorne come from Dougall (Gaelic, 'dark foreigner'), grandson of Norse King Olaf, the Black. Some clans are linked with ancient monastic houses: the Macnabs, 'son of the abbot', descend from lay abbots of St Fillan on Loch Earn; the Macleans in Morven come from Gillean, who descended from the abbots of Lismore, the island in Loch Linnhe. Other examples include Macmillan, 'son of a tonsured man'; Buchanan, 'of the canon's house'; MacTaggart, 'son of a priest', and MacPherson, 'son of a parson'. Clans with uncertain origins include the MacKenzies who appeared in Ross and Cromarty, claiming descent from twelfth-century kinsman Gilleoin, as do the Mathesons, with lands close to Kyleakin in Wester Ross. The Gunns in Sutherland claim a most unusual descent: they may have been an ancient surviving Pictish tribe, forced into the far north of Scotland.

THE LORDS OF THE ISLES

Clan Donald, the Lords of the Isles, were for generations the most powerful clan in Scotland, especially on the lands by the western seaboard. Great seafarers, they controlled the sea lanes with their oared galleys (Gaelic: *birlinn*) about which there were many songs and tales. The power of Clan Donald was finally broken before the end of the fifteenth century, their power having brought them into conflict with the Crown.

THE MASSACRE OF GLENCOE

Clan conflict often meant spilt blood. The MacGregors are said to have massacred 140 of the Colquhouns in Glen Fruin, west of Loch Lomond. Clan Donald forces once shut a hundred Campbells in a barn near Oban and set it alight. More than a hundred Lamonts were executed at Dunoon in revenge for changing sides by the Campbells after the Battle of Inverlochy. Yet the bloody deed which has gained most notoriety was not principally a clan affair. The Massacre of Glencoe (1692) was carried out on a branch of the Clan Donald by a regular regiment of the 'British' army, raised from the Clan Campbell. The Campbell regiment acted under orders as part of a government policy designed to bring rebel clans to heel. In this case, the brutal politics of the late seventeenth century was far more important than simple clan enmity.

THE CLANS AT CULLODEN

The powerful Clan Campbell were to the fore at the Battle of Culloden in 1746 as well. Their militia took the government side against the 5,000 rebel Jacobites and were part of the 9,000-strong British army which included three other regiments of Lowland Scots. Subsequent Jacobite mythology has obscured the fact that more Scots took up arms against Bonnie Prince Charlie than for him. The popular interpretation of Culloden as a Scotland–England conflict is simply a myth.

THE CLAN REVIVAL AND THE CLANS TODAY

As part of a Romantic movement in art and literature in the late eighteenth century, an interest in nature began to take root both north and south of the border. The first tourists came to Scotland, as part of a 'cult of the picturesque' which began to spring up. Another aspect of the Romantic movement was an interest in the idea of 'the noble savage' and thus a certain mystique began to spring up around the Highlands, which had been populated by a race of noble warriors. This new way of thinking, embodied in the work of Sir Walter Scott with his tales of Scottish heroes and brave deeds, received wide acclaim. In addition, by the end of the eighteenth century the Highlands were no longer seen as a threat to the nation's stability, Scotland becoming safe enough for a visit by the reigning monarch, King George IV, in 1822. The old clan ways had been swept aside by emigration, proscription following Culloden, the Industrial Revolution and 'foreign' landlords, who all changed the nature of clans and clan lands. Queen Victoria's love of the Highlands and Balmoral and her patronage of the Braemar Highland Gathering helped sustain the fashion and the genuine interest in Scotland's Highland heritage. This has been maintained to the present day, often taking the form of clan societies which promote the history and comradeship of the clan. Though the clans of old have gone from their homelands forever, the old traditional values of loyalty and companionship still have their place, within a family that now stretches right round the world.

IMMIGRATION AND EMIGRATION

Although there has been both immigration to and emigration from Scotland on a fairly large scale, there are actually very few records of this movement of population.

There are ship passenger lists, but these only commence in 1890 and are in the Public Record Office in London. If your interest lies in emigrants before this date, as is more than likely, there are various published lists covering emigrants to Canada and the United States, which have been compiled from various sources and are listed in the Bibliography. Having checked these, your next course of action would be to consult the immigration records of the country of destination. We recommend you check the Ellis Island Web site (www.ellisisland.org) if you are interested in the period 1892–1924, since this searches on over twenty-two million individuals who entered the United States of America via Ellis Island between those dates.

IRISH IMMIGRATION

During the first half of the nineteenth century in particular there was a considerable influx of Irish people into Scotland, with the main destinations being Glasgow, Edinburgh and Dundee. It can be very difficult to trace the place of origin of these immigrants since the census records only record the birthplace as Ireland. The most useful source is the Poor Relief Applications which record the birthplaces of many Irish people in Scotland; this gives an added value to the Database in the Glasgow City Archives since Glasgow had the largest concentration of Irish immigrants in Scotland.

As mentioned already in Chapter 6, Glasgow City Archives has computerised indexes for Lanarkshire and Dunbartonshire covering the period 1855–1900, with another for Renfrewshire in preparation. The Ardrossan and Kilmarnock Poor Law records have been indexed on computer for part of the nineteenth century, being available at the East Ayrshire Family History Society and Glasgow and West of Scotland Family History Society's premises. All the names, not just the applicants, have been indexed in this case and the Ardrossan records are also a good source for information on Irish immigrants.

Other significant groups who arrived in Scotland in the eighteenth and nineteenth centuries were of Jewish and Italian origin.

JEWISH IMMIGRATION

The Scottish Jewish Archive Centre collects a wide range of material relating to all aspects of the history of the Jewish communities of

Scotland and is located in Garnethill Synagogue – the oldest in Scotland, built in 1879.

Their large collection is catalogued on computer, and made available to researchers.

The Historical Database of Scottish Jewry, available at the Scottish Jewish Archives Centre, collates and cross-references a wide variety of sources and lists – some sixty lists and sources, including cemetery records, synagogue registers, naturalisations, charity subscription lists and school admission registers – relating to Jews in Scotland up to the 1920s. It has information on almost 16,500 individuals, and continues to grow. This database is the most comprehensive source for those who are trying to locate individuals and families during this period.

For further Jewish genealogical information and links, consult the Web site of the Jewish Genealogical Society of Great Britain (www.jgsgb.org.uk).

ITALIAN IMMIGRATION

Italian immigration into Scotland began in the nineteenth century, but by 1890 the numbers totalled only about 750. However, by 1914 this had increased to about 4,500. Many of these 'Scots–Italians' ran small businesses as owners of cafes and ice-cream parlours and tended to form themselves into distinct communities, often inter-marrying.

For further Scottish–Italian information and links, there is currently a Web site concerned with Scots–Italian interests (www. members.lycos.co.uk/scots_italian).

The following two sections provide some of the historical background to the most usual destinations for emigrants from Scotland – the Americas, Australia and New Zealand.

EMIGRATION TO THE AMERICAS

The Scottish participation in the settlement of America dates from the early seventeenth century, and from that time until the American Revolution probably around 150,000 Scots emigrated to the New World. During the seventeenth century many Scots settled within the English, Dutch and French colonies, while others attempted to establish independent Scots colonies in Nova Scotia, New Jersey, South Carolina and at Darien (now known as Panama).

While many Scots emigrated for their own reasons, the majority of Scots arrived in colonial America against their will. The first group of Covenanters banished from Great Britain arrived in America in the late seventeenth century. As the clan chiefs became wealthier and more powerful, they grew more distant from the clan members who farmed the land and fought the battles. The clan chiefs discovered Cheviot and Blackface sheep and realised that they could make more money raising sheep than they could from the farmers. Since there was now more law and government, they no longer needed to maintain large clans for their own protection. They could use only two or three peasants to care for the sheep and be rid of the headaches caused by being responsible for the safety and welfare of the hundreds who had lived on the lands for years. They called it 'agricultural improvement' and began to drive the clan members from their land by charging very high rent or by forceably evicting them. These farming people moved to the towns of Scotland, Ireland or England to seek jobs but since the labour market was flooded, most were unsuccessful. Some went to the coast to become fishermen, but again they found little work. They emigrated simply to support themselves and some had to come as indentured servants in order to pay their fares.

Eventually, people under the king's rule had to swear allegiance to him and his authority. Jacobites and Covenanters, of course, refused on political and religious grounds, so they were transported to the New World (colonial America, Canada, Jamaica, Antigua, and so on). Since the ports of the American east coast received so many immigrant ships, the Scots settled in the east, but primarily in the south. Like later immigrants, they tended to settle where others of their culture had established colonies, so relatively large numbers of Scots stayed in the agrarian south and established new lives here.

Beginning in 1716, Jacobite Highlanders were banished to the Americas. Continuing persecution encouraged other Scots to emigrate well into the nineteenth century.

After the political union of Scotland and England in 1707, the Scots had unrestricted access to the English plantations in America. Emigration expanded slowly but steadily until 1763 when a combination of factors in Scotland and America stimulated emigration, especially from the Highlands. Although Scots could be found throughout the American colonies from Barbados to Rupert's Land, areas such as Georgia, the Carolinas, upper New York, Nova Scotia and Jamaica had the greatest concentration of Scottish immigrants.

This then was the general pattern of Scottish immigration and settlement in colonial America.

EMIGRATION TO AUSTRALIA AND NEW ZEALAND

Following the peace of 1815 at the end of the Napoleonic Wars, there was a great increase in the population of the British Isles. A growing population, which had previously been regarded as one of the nation's strengths, now began to be looked on as something of a curse.

Perhaps the easiest remedy was emigration. Though most of the emigrants chosen for Government-assisted passages in these early years were Irish, many Scots were also attracted by the offers of free land overseas.

Despite its reputation as a penal colony, in the very early years of the nineteenth century, Australia had begun to appear more and more as a practical proposition for settlement (only three per cent of the deported convicts had been Scottish). After the United States had won its independence, Australia slowly began to offer an alternative to the vast wildernesses of loyalist Canada.

Although Tasmania (then known as Van Dieman's Land) was the main destination of the first Scottish emigrants, many also went to New South Wales. The populations of both colonies rose by one third during the 1820s. The 1827 publication of Scotsman Peter Cunningham's *Two Years in New South Wales* painted a picture that was irresistible to many – a free land with available unpaid convict labour, where a staple export, merino wool, was already developing rapidly.

A wave of emigration from Scotland then began. Who could not have been enticed by reports in the *Edinburgh Courant* of a land with 'the climate of Italy, the mountain scenery of Wales and the fertility of England'? Later editions reporting 'distress, moral misery and vice' were conveniently ignored. There were too many opportunities available in Van Dieman's Land. Notable early arrivals were the Imlay Brothers from Aberdeenshire who soon owned large properties and businesses. In 1839, Melbourne was described as a 'Scotch settlement'. Pockets of Scottish communities were formed throughout the mainland. Among the first to settle in Queensland was a Scots family, the Archers.

As Scotland, and Edinburgh in particular, held a high reputation for its educational institutions, many of which specialised in medicine, it is no wonder that among the surgeon-superintendents of the early convict ships, Scots figured prominently. Many of these doctors applied for land grants and continued their professions as civilians. Other groups to become prominent, in addition to retired army officers, small merchants and farmers, were surveyors and engineers, landowners, distillers, brewers, shipbuilders and manufacturers.

More than one historian has pointed out the 'high quality' of the early Scots settlers. A large influx of poorer classes of Scottish settlers did not arrive until the bounty schemes at the end of the 1830s. Those who came earlier were much more prepared to undergo risks, utilise resources and aspire to commercial enterprise on a large scale.

The Australian Company of Edinburgh was formed in 1822 to explore trading possibilities with Australia. Early on, the company's successful activities and strong links with Australia served to encourage many Scots to emigrate to that country in order to take a more active part in trading with their fellows back home, however the Company was forced to disband in the 1830s because Canada and Nova Scotia were attracting most of the Scottish settlers.

A large-scale movement of emigration from Scotland began after 1832 just as the country had entered the most important phase of its industrial revolution.

The huge increase of population that accompanied industrial progress meant that no part of Scotland was now unaffected by the rush to emigrate. Social upheaval probably had as much to do with it as the availability of free or assisted passages to Australia after 1832. Economic setbacks in the late 1830s and early 1840s also contributed to the outward flow of emigrant ships from Scottish ports.

A new class of emigrants streamed into the colony, this time drawn from the near-destitute working class, aided by the Government's bounty system. In 1831, Lord Gooderich initiated the system for assisted female emigration to New South Wales. This was expanded in 1835 when an additional scheme encouraged the emigration of skilled agricultural workers in addition to unmarried women and mechanics. In 1837, the number of Scots leaving for Australia began to match those leaving for North America.

Many of those who left were Highlanders. An August 1838 letter sent from a Scottish settler in Van Dieman's Land shows only too well the reasons why poor Highland families, already dispossessed in the mad rush to enclose lands to benefit their lairds, were taking their meagre transportable belongings and heading for the nearest port of embarkation:

'However his love of country, the man who prefers a dear farm and a life of unrequited toil amid the bleak cold mountains of Caledonia to the certain and almost immediate prospects which this country holds out to him, cannot be under the guidance of reason.'

The economic crisis of 1841–2 ended the government bounty system. As Irish emigration was almost two-thirds of the total from the British Isles during the period in question, the importance of the Scottish contribution to so many areas of Australian life becomes even more marked. One outstanding example out of so many is that of Sir James McCulloch, who left Scotland in 1853 to open a branch office in Melbourne for his mercantile firm and who became minister of trade and customs and treasurer in 1859, progressing to prime minister of Victoria in 1863.

Other Scots became equally successful in New Zealand, Britain's other colony 'down under'. It was another area chosen to alleviate Scotland's growing population in the early nineteenth century. In fact, if we discount the native Maori peoples, the most striking difference between the population of the British Isles and New Zealand is the great over-representation of Scots in the latter. In the mid-nineteenth century, Scots made up a quarter of New Zealand's population.

The Scots have been described as being to New Zealand what the Irish were to Australia. One historian has seen them as 'the chief lieutenants of settlement' in those beautiful Pacific islands. Though a huge number of Irish people emigrated to Australia, it was New Zealand that drew the majority of Scots. In peak years, more than one third of all Scots emigrants went to New Zealand. At first, they clustered in Otago and its offshoot, Sutherland, in the South Island. Both places were half-Scottish in 1871.

In proportion to its population, financial strength and available resources, the contribution of the Scots to the commercial development of Australia and New Zealand was far greater than that of any other people of the British Isles.

HERALDRY

Heraldry, the system by which individuals and, later, organisations can be identified by a symbol known as 'arms' or 'coats of arms', developed in the twelfth century throughout Europe into a fairly standardised system. Particularly important was the fact that these arms were inherited. The original purpose was, of course, to allow noble warriors and their supporters to be identified in battle, where the arms could appear on shields, banners and tunics. Another use was on seals, authenticating important documents. Usage spread far beyond this and became a very popular means of personalising possessions, ranging from silverware and furniture to buildings.

Although only a small proportion of the population is 'armigerous', that is, has the right to use arms, you may perhaps discover at some point in your researches that you have a connection to an individual using arms. Association with a particular clan also brings up the question of the appropriate use of arms, crests and badges linked to the clan name. This section aims to give you a basic understanding of this system and how it interrelates to family history.

First, it is important to be clear about some of the basic elements of heraldry. What is meant by the arms or coat of arms, the crest and the badge and how are they used?

The arms are the symbol or symbols forming a complete design, belonging to one individual, which is used on a shield, banner, tunic or elsewhere. The term crest is often incorrectly used to describe the arms, but only refers to a device which sits on top of a helmet placed above a shield. Not all those bearing arms have a crest, but those who do may use it in addition to or as an alternative to their arms as a mark of personalisation. The badge, as used in Scotland, consists of a crest, surrounded by a circular strap with a buckle, which usually displays a motto. This can be worn by the supporters of the individual whose crest it features and many examples are seen in the various clan badges.

Next we will look at the various elements which can make up the arms, which can range from the simplest of designs to a complex but meaningful combination of many symbols. The 'field' is the name given to the complete area of the shield and forms the foundation of all coats of arms. On this is placed one of the tinctures. The tinctures consist of the following: five colours – azure (blue), gules (red), purpure (purple), sable (black) and vert (green); two metals – argent (silver) and or (gold); not so often found, three stains – murrey (mulberry), sanguine (blood red) and tenne (tawny orange); and the 'furs' – ermine (with variations) and vair (with variations). The reproduction of the tinctures can vary, with shades ranging from pale blue to navy in the case of azure, while argent and or are usually rendered as white and yellow. There is a general rule that one colour is not placed on another, nor a metal placed on another metal. This helps to maintain a good contrast in the design, but is not adhered to rigidly. The ermine furs have a pattern of spots and tails using black on white, white on black, black on gold or gold on black. The vair furs appear normally in white and blue, using a pattern based on squirrel skins. Each of these varieties of fur has its own name.

Once this background has been established, the next stage in creating the coat of arms involves placing 'ordinaries', 'subordinaries' and 'charges' on the shield.

The ordinaries are large, simple shapes. The following are the most commonly used ordinaries:

- Pale (broad vertical band).
- Fess (broad horizontal band).
- Bend (broad diagonal band).
- Chief (broad band across top of shield).
- Cross.
- Saltire (X-shaped cross).
- Pile (V-shaped triangle).
- Chevron (broad inverted V-shape).
- Pall (Y-shape).

Only one ordinary, if any, would normally be used, but a chief is often combined with another ordinary. It is also possible to have a number of these shapes in a smaller form – 'diminutives'. The shield can be divided up by these shapes, for example per pale divides the shield vertically in two parts.

The subordinaries are other geometric shapes, which, unlike the ordinaries, can be used in multiples. The bordure (wide border) is one of these, others being roundels (circles) and the inescutcheon (small shield in centre of main shield).

Charges could be anything else to be put on the shield. Animals and birds are commonly found charges.

Another means of varying the design is to use different types of line in dividing up a shield or outlining ordinaries and subordinaries.

Once the design of the arms is complete, it should be able to be described in a 'blazon' of the arms, that is, a standardised form of description in old French, traditionally used by heralds. First comes the field, then the ordinaries, subordinaries, charges and, finally, a chief or bordure, if present, and any device to be placed over the rest of the design.

It is most important to remember the principle that a coat of arms is personal to one individual. It follows from this that most arms are 'differenced'. Eldest sons inherit the arms of their fathers, but even they require differenced arms during their fathers' lifetimes.

Marks of cadency provide differences between the arms of various individuals within the same family. Some of the most commonly found are the label (a horizontal bar with three downward tabs for an eldest son, or with five tabs for a grandson), the crescent for a second son, and the molet (five-pointed star) for a third son. Once the younger sons had established their own households, they were obliged to register officially differenced coats of arms with the Court of the Lord Lyon King of Arms. These arms were often differenced by the use of variously coloured borders.

WOMEN AND ARMS

Women usually displayed arms on a lozenge rather than a shield and were entitled to use their fathers' arms. During their married life they could 'impale' these (place them side by side) with their husbands' arms if they wished. As widows, they could also use their husbands' arms. If a woman had no brothers living, or children of brothers, she had a right to use the arms of her father, either undifferenced, if she was the eldest daughter, or differenced. If the eldest daughter, she could, being an heiress, pass her arms on to her children who could 'quarter' her arms with their father's, displaying the father's arms in the first and fourth quarters of the shield and the mother's in the second and third quarters. Sometimes individuals ended up with numerous 'quarterings' on their arms.

Responsibility for all matters heraldic in Scotland lies with the Lord Lyon King of Arms and the administration is undertaken by the Lyon Court. These matters are strictly regulated and, unlike the situation in England, all differenced versions of arms must be registered in the Lyon Court, which maintains 'The Public register of all arms and bearings in Scotland' dating from 1672. This contains a considerable amount of genealogical information on the ancestry of those registering arms. Two published volumes provide details of arms from the register covering 1672–1972. In addition to this, the Lyon Office records include the 'register of genealogies' covering 1727–96 and 1823 to the present, but due to the high cost of registering genealogies, this was not used extensively. Also there are records of birth briefs, funeral entries and funeral escutcheons, again available in published form (see the Bibliography). If you wish to pursue the study of heraldry further, you should consult the works listed in the Bibliography.

ENGLISH, WELSH AND IRISH RECORDS

ENGLISH AND WELSH RECORDS

The Civil Registers in England do begin earlier (1837) than those in Scotland, but provide less information. For example, the marriage certificates only give the names of the fathers of the bride and groom and the death certificates do not give any parents' names at all.

The procedure for searching the Civil Registers is also quite different. The indexes only are available at the Family Records Centre in London and if you find an entry which you are interested in, you must then apply for an official copy of the certificate. Searching in this way can take very much longer than a day's general search in New Register House, where you can verify entries as you go.

CENSUS RECORDS

There is little to say about the census records since these are virtually the same as those for Scotland and are also kept in the Family Records Centre. As already described in Chapter 3, the 1881 British Census on CD-ROM covers England and Wales as well as Scotland. The English and Welsh portion is also available online on the Family Search Web site.

The 1901 census for England and Wales is now available on the Web, the index being searchable free of charge. Should you wish to access the full details, a charge is made.

INTERNATIONAL GENEALOGICAL INDEX

The IGI is available on microfiche divided up by county and on the Internet on the Family Search Web site, but the coverage is rather patchy.

When we come to the earlier records, we see a contrast between the centralisation of many of the Scottish sources in New Register House and the National Archives of Scotland and the decentralisation in England and Wales, with much being kept in the local archives or record offices. In particular, the parish registers are held in the local offices. Many more of these have earlier starting dates than in Scotland, with 1538 or 1558 being fairly common.

WILLS AND ADMINISTRATIONS

Other major soursces are wills and administrations, marriage licences and land records. Wills and administrations (granted for those not leaving a will) are stored centrally at the Probate Department of The Principal Probate Registry Family Division, London, from 1858, but before that may be found in several locations. For more information on how to locate these you could consult *Probate Jurisdictions: Where to Look for Wills* by Jeremy Gibson (2002). The Public Record Office on their Documents Online Web site are making the index to the Prerogative Court of Canterbury wills available. Entries for the period 1650–1858 are currently being added. Copies of these wills can be downloaded for a standard charge of £3.

MARRIAGE LICENCES

In Scotland, marriages were authorised by the proclamation of banns, but in England there was the alternative of having a marriage licence granted. These are found mainly in local archives or record offices and some have been published. Often they give the occupation of the groom and names the place or places where the marriage might take place. In a situation where one or both of the couple were under age, the consent of the parents would be required and so in most cases the father's name would be given.

LAND RECORDS

These are nothing like as complete as in Scotland. The main sources are the manorial court rolls which have survived for some areas, but are haphazard compared to the sasines.

The Origins Web site now makes available several useful databases, including parts of Boyd's Marriage Index, an important source for many parts of England. Payment is needed to access these indexes.

IRISH RECORDS

To begin with, the bad news. Unfortunately many Irish records were lost in 1922 when the four courts in Dublin were destroyed. Amongst these were almost all Irish wills and about 1,000 Protestant church registers of baptisms, marriages and burials. Now let's look at what does survive.

Civil Registration began in 1864, giving the same information as English Civil Registration but Protestant marriages had been registered from 1845.

All these records are in the General Register Office of Ireland in Dublin, except for the Civil Registers covering Northern Ireland from 1922, which are in the General Register Office (Northern Ireland) in Belfast.

CENSUS RECORDS

Unlike the rest of the British Isles, the census records for 1901 and 1911 are open to the public and fairly complete, but before this, little exists. The various Web sites on Irish family history give details of earlier census fragments and 'census substitutes'. All Census records are held in the National Archives in Dublin.

Because of the lack of these records, two sets of land records have assumed greater importance, the Tithe Applotment books and Griffith's Valuation. The Tithe Applotment books, compiled in the period 1823 to 1838, give the names of the occupiers of lands, the area of land and the tithes payable to the Church of Ireland. These are not comprehensive, however. Griffith's Valuation, published between 1848 and 1864, gives a valuation of all property in Ireland, listing the names and addresses of all occupiers of land and householders. This should be available in large reference libraries.

CHURCH REGISTERS

The coverage of church registers is not good, with only a few Roman Catholic registers from before 1820. There are microfilm copies of these in the National Library of Ireland, Dublin. For the Church of Ireland, the Irish branch of the Anglican Church, about 600 registers have survived and are held by the local churches, or in the Public Record Office, Dublin. It is advisable to check with the Church of Ireland in Dublin for further details. Many of the Presbyterian church records are held by either the local churches or the Presbyterian Historical Society in Belfast.

WILLS

Although very many of these were destroyed, the situation is not quite as bad as it might seem at first. There is an index published in 1897 entitled 'Index to the Prerogative Wills of Ireland, 1536–1810' by Vicars and also the Betham extracts of wills – extracts of genealogical information from almost all wills proved in the Prerogative Court of Armagh, 1536–1800. These are mainly confined to wills of those with property in more than one diocese. There are copies of these extracts in the National Archives, Dublin and the Genealogical Office, also in Dublin.

The indexes of wills and administrations proved in the consistory courts and the Prerogative Court up to 1857 have survived and are in the National Archives.

From 1858 onwards there are indexes of wills and administrations in the National Archives in Dublin and the Public Record Office of Northern Ireland, giving the date and place of death and occupation of the individual along with the names and addresses of the executors. Some copies of wills for this period are also available at these two repositories.

MARRIAGE LICENCES

The prerogative marriage licences for 1630–1858 and the Ossory consistory licences, 1734–1808 are kept in the Genealogical Office, in Dublin.

Indexes for about a dozen dioceses, covering the period up to 1857, are available in the National Archives in Dublin, while some have been printed up to 1800.

MONUMENTAL INSCRIPTIONS

As in Scotland, many inscriptions have been recorded and published and can prove a useful source.

Origins provides free Web access to over 24,000 Irish genealogy Web pages, including census data, Griffith's Valuation, and so on and is worth consulting.

INTERPRETING OLDER FORMS OF HANDWRITING

As your researches take you back in time, the problem of reading the handwriting becomes more acute, because, although even relatively recent documents may sometimes be difficult to read, in earlier documents you have different forms of letters and even sometimes different languages to contend with.

The most common style of handwriting used in official documents from about 1600 to about 1750 was 'secretary hand'. Some of the common letter forms are different from those of today, in particular the letters e, h, r and s.

It has been stated by Johnson and Jenkinson in their *English Court Hand* (1915) that 'it is not too much to say that you cannot read a word with certainty unless you know what it is.' To achieve this, try to familiarise yourself with the type of document you will be reading, for example parish register, Kirk session records, a testament, a sasine. It may well follow a standard format, including abbreviations. You may find it helpful to refer to a Scots and perhaps a Latin dictionary, legal word lists and glossaries. It is even more important to build up this background knowledge if you are tackling documents in Latin.

Despite what we have just said, do not be put off by feeling there is a tremendous amount of study to be undertaken before even starting to read a document. If you are unable to spend this time, it is still often possible to achieve a lot through sheer perseverance.

PROBLEM WORDS

These may occur for several reasons:

- **Interference** may be caused by descending letters from above or ascending letters from below. Be careful not to regard these as part of the word you are trying to decipher.

- **Abbreviations.** Widespread use was made of these in earlier times. There may be tell-tale marks indicating that an abbreviation has been used. A 'mark of suspension' shows where letters are missing from the end of a word. The mark is usually a flourish from the last written letter. A 'mark of contraction' shows where letters are missing from the middle of a word. This mark is usually above the line. Common omissions are the letters m and n. Words beginning with p may be abbreviations for the prefixes pro, pre or per. A superscript letter could also indicate an abbreviation, especially after the now obsolete letter 'thorn', for example Yt = that.
- **Different spellings.** Remember that spelling in the past was not standardised as it is today, so be prepared for variant spellings.
- **Non-English words.** There could be Scots words or Latin words and for these you might want to consult Scots or Latin dictionaries.
- **Legal terms.** You could consult the SCAN glossary or books mentioned in the Bibliography.
- **Numerals.** These are usually written as Roman numerals and if there is an i at the end of the numeral, it appears as a j.
- **Dates.** Sometimes you may find a year written in a strange mixture of Roman numerals and words. This includes the use of three elements, firstly jaj, meaning, 1000, secondly the Roman numeral v, vi or vij (5, 6 or 7) and C (for 100) with a mark of contraction, then the rest in words, e.g. jajvijC + twentie (1720).

It is a good idea to compare individual words and letters to see whether they are more legible elsewhere in the document. The context in which a word appears can also help in working out a difficult word. Try putting the document aside for a time and return to it later, when a second reading may fill in gaps from the first reading. With practice you will find that you become more accustomed to reading old documents.

For further help in the study of handwriting, or palaeography, you could consult the books listed in the Bibliography and the Scottish Handwriting Web site. Courses are also available on the subject.

APPENDIX 3

WEB SITES

See pp. 67–78 for details of some of these sites.

ARCHIVES

A2A (Accesss to Archives)
http://www.a2a.pro.gov.uk

Aberdeen City Archives
http://www.aberdeencity.gov.uk/archivists.htm

Angus Archives
http://www.angus.gov.uk/history/history.htm

Archives Hub
http://www.archiveshub.ac.uk

Archivesinfo: UK Archival Repositories on the Internet.
http://www.archivesinfo.net/uksites.html

Ayrshire Archives Centre
http://www.south-ayrshire.gov.uk/Archives/

Bank of Scotland: Archives
http://www.bankofscotland.co.uk/info/archives/archives-info.html

Clackmannanshire Council Archives
http://www.clacksweb.org.uk/dyna/archives

Dumfries and Galloway Archives
http://www.dumgal.gov.uk/services/depts/comres/library/archives.htm

Dundee City Archive and Record Centre
http://www.dundeecity.gov.uk/dcchtml/sservices/archives.html

East Dunbartonshire Information and Archives
http://www.eastdunbarton.gov.uk (search under archives)

Edinburgh City Archives
  http://www.edinburgh.gov.uk/CEC/Corporate_Services/
  Corporate_Communications/archivist/Edinburgh_City_
  Archives.html

Family Records Centre
  http://www.pro.gov.uk/about/access/frc.htm

The General Register Office, Dublin
  http://www.groireland.ie

General Register Office for England and Wales, Postal Application
Section
  http://www.statistics.gov.uk/nsbase/registration/certificates.asp

General Register Office for Northern Ireland
  http://www.groni.gov.uk

General Register Office for Scotland
  http://www.gro-scotland.gov.uk

Glasgow Archdiocese (Roman Catholic), Archdiocesan Archive
  http://www.rcag.org.uk/Archives/Index.htm

Glasgow City Archives
  http://www.mitchelllibrary.org/archives.htm

Glasgow University. University of Glasgow Archive Services
  http://www.archives.gla.ac.uk

Greater Glasgow NHS Board Archive
  http://www.archives.gla.ac.uk/gghb

Highland Council Archive
  http://www.highland.gov.uk/cl/publicservices/archivedetails/
  highlandarchive.htm

Historical Manuscripts Commission
  http://www.hmc.gov.uk

Land Registry and Registry of Deeds, Dublin
  http://www.irlgov.ie/landreg

Lothian Health Services Archive
  http://www.lhsa.lib.ed.ac.uk

Memorial University, Newfoundland: Maritime History Archive
  http://www.mun.ca/mha/genealog.html

Moray Council Local Heritage Centre
http://www.moray.org/heritage/index.html

The National Archives of Ireland, Dublin
http://www.nationalarchives.ie/genealogy.html

National Archives of Scotland
http://www.nas.gov.uk

National Library of Ireland
http://www.heanet.ie/natlib/index.html

National Maritime Museum, London – merchant seamen
http://www.nmm.ac.uk

National Register of Archives
http://www.hmc.gov.uk/nra/nra2.htm

North Highland Archive
http://www.highland.gov.uk/cl/publicservices/archivedetails/
northarchive.htm

Perth and Kinross Council Archive
http://www.pkc.gov.uk/library/archive.htm

Principal Registry of the Family Division
http://www.courtservice.gov.uk/fandl/prob_guidance.htm

Public Record Office
http://www.pro.gov.uk

Public Record Office of Northern Ireland
http://proni.nics.gov.uk/index.htm

Registers of Scotland
http://www.ros.gov.uk

Registrar of Births, Deaths and Marriages (Dundee)
http://www.dundeecity.gov.uk/registrars

Royal Bank of Scotland Archive
http://www.rbs.co.uk/group_info/memorybank

Royal College of Physicians and Surgeons of Glasgow
http://www.rcpsglasg.ac.uk/archives.htm

Royal College of Physicians of Edinburgh
http://www.rcpe.ac.uk/library/index.html

Royal College of Surgeons of Edinburgh
http://www.rcsed.ac.uk/geninfo/library/Default.asp

Scottish Archive Network
   http://www.scan.org.uk

Signet Library
   http://www.signetlibrary.co.uk/library.htm

West Lothian Council, Archives and Records Management Unit
   http://www.wlonline.org/Site/Living/library/archives/default.htm

BACKGROUND

Statistical Accounts of Scotland 1791–9 and 1845
   http://edina.ac.uk/StatAcc

BIBLIOGRAPHIES

Bibliography of Scotland – part of Scottish Bibliographies Online
   http://sbo.nls.uk/cgi-bin/Pwebrecon.cgi?DB=local&PAGE=First

BIOGRAPHIES

World Biographical Index – includes British Biographical Index
   http://www.saur-wbi.de

CLANS

The Gathering of the Clans
   http://www.tartans.com

COMPUTERS

BBC Internet Introduction
   http://www.bbc.co.uk/webwise

Beginners' Central – basic course on Internet use
   http://www.northernwebs.com/bc

Computers in genealogy – journal
   http://www.sog.org.uk/cig

Family Tree Maker
   http://familytreemaker.genealogy.com

Generations Family Tree
   http://www.sierrahome.com

MyFamily.com – Internet community for families
   http://www.myfamily.com

Personal Ancestral File (PAF) – free download
http://www.familysearch.org

Reunion
http://www.leisterpro.com

TONIC – basic course on Internet use
http://www.netskills.ac.uk/TonicNG/cgi/sesame?tng

Ultimate Family Tree
http://www.ultimatefamilytree.com

EMIGRATION AND IMMIGRATION

Dobson, David
http://www.users.zetnet.co.uk/dobson.genealogy

Ellis Island Web site
http://www.ellisisland.org

Jewish Genealogical Society of Great Britain
http://www.jgsgb.org.uk

Scotsitalian.co.uk
http://members.lycos.co.uk/scots_italian

FAMILY HISTORY GUIDES

Familyrecords.gov: family history guides – page of links
http://www.familyrecords.gov.uk/guides.htm

Family Tree Maker's Genealogy Site – free genealogy classes
http://familytreemaker.genealogy.com/university.html?Welcome
=1019077854

Vermont College, USA – Learn family history online
http://www.tui.edu/vermontcollege/lifelong/family.html

GENERAL GENEALOGY SITES

Ancestry.com
http://ancestry.com

Cyndi's List of genealogy sites on the Internet
http://www.CyndisList.com

RootsWeb.com
http://www.rootsweb.com

Strathclyde University Library – Scottish Family History
http://www.strath.ac.uk/Departments/JHLibrary/scotfam.html

GENETICS

DeCODE Genetics
http://www.decode.com

Estonian Genome Foundation
http://www.genomics.ee

Family Tree DNA
http://www.familytreedna.com

Oxford Ancestors
http://www.oxfordancestors.com

HANDWRITING

Scottish Handwriting
http://www.scottishhandwriting.com

HISTORICAL DEMOGRAPHY

Cambridge Group for the History of Population and Social Structure
http://www-hpss.geog.cam.ac.uk

LIBRARY CATALOGUES

British Library Public Catalogue
http://blpc.bl.uk

BUBL UK: libraries
http://bubl.ac.uk/uk/libraries.htm

CAIRNS
http://cairns.lib.strath.ac.uk

COPAC
http://www.copac.ac.uk

Library of Congress (USA) Online Catalog
http://catalog.loc.gov

National Library of Scotland
http://www.nls.uk

MAILING LISTS AND FORUMS

Cyndi's List – mailing lists
http://www.CyndisList.com/mailing.htm

GENBRIT – mailing list for British genealogy
http://lists.rootsweb.com/index/intl/UK/GENBRIT.html

GenForum – host to thousands of mailing lists
http://genforum.genealogy.com

RootsWeb mailing lists
http://lists.rootsweb.com

ORIGINAL SOURCES

1851 Co. Antrim Census – remains of the census
http://irishgenealogy.net/antrimgen.html#CENSUS2

Ayrshire towns in Pigot's Directory 1837
http://www.ayrshireroots.com/Genealogy/Reference/1837%20
Ayrshire/Ayrshire%20Directories.htm

The Commonwealth War Graves Commission
http://www.cwgc.org

Ellis Island Web site
http://www.ellisisland.org

Family Research Link – copy of the indexes of births, marriages and
deaths for England and Wales from 1837 to 2001 available on a pay
per view basis.
http://www.1837online.com/

Family Search Internet genealogy service
http://www.familysearch.org

FreeBMD – RootsWeb project
http://freebmd.rootsweb.com

FreeCEN – RootsWeb project
http://freecen.rootsweb.com

FreeREG – RootsWeb project
http://freereg.rootsweb.com

Glasgow Street Directory 1787
http://www.britishislesgenweb.org/scotland/archives
http://www.ayrshireroots.com/Genealogy/Historical/Jones%20
Directory.htm

Origins.net
http://www.origins.net

Scotland's People
http://www.scotlandspeople.gov.uk

Scottish documents – index of Scottish wills to 1901
http://www.scottishdocuments.com

PRESENTATION

Crawfurd of Jordanhill family tree
http://www.strath.ac.uk/Departments/JHLibrary/archives/
crawfurdtree.html

Timperley of Hintlesham
http://homepages.strath.ac.uk/~cjis19/timp.htm

SEARCH ENGINES/DIRECTORIES

Dogpile – metacrawler
http://www.dogpile.com/index.gsp

Google – search engine
http://www.google.co.uk

Ixquick – metacrawler
http://www.ixquick.com

Search Engine Watch
http://searchenginewatch.com

Yahoo – Internet directory
http://www.yahoo.com

SOCIETIES AND ASSOCIATIONS

Aberdeen and North East Scotland Family History Society
http://www.anesfhs.force9.co.uk/index.htm

Alloway and Southern Ayrshire Family History Society
http://www.maybole.org/history/resources/asafhs.htm

Anglo-Scottish Family History Society
http://www.mlfhs.demon.co.uk/AngloScots

Association of Scottish Genealogists and Record Agents (ASGRA)
http://www.asgra.co.uk

Borders Family History Society
http://www.vivdunstan.clara.net/genuki/misc/bordersFHS.html

Catholic Family History Society
http://www.feefhs.org/uk/frg-cfhs.html

Central Scotland Family History Society
http://www.CSFHS.org.uk

Dumfries and Galloway Family History Society
http://www.dgfhs.org.uk

East Ayrshire Family History Society
http://www.eastayrshirefhs.org.uk

Federation of Family History Societies
http://www.ffhs.org.uk

Fife Family History Society
http://www.fifefhs.pwp.blueyonder.co.uk

Glasgow and West of Scotland Family History Society
http://www.gwsfhs.org.uk

Guild of One-Name Studies
http://www.one-name.org

Highland Family History Society
http://www.genuki.org.uk/big/scot/Highland.FHS.home.html

Jewish Genealogical Society of Great Britain
http://www.jgsgb.org.uk

Lanarkshire Family History Society
http://www.lanarkshirefhs.org.uk

Largs and North Ayrshire Family History Society
http://lnafhs.freeyellow.com/index.html

Lothians Family History Society
http://www.btinternet.com/%7Emmgene/lfhs

Orkney Family History Society
http://www.genuki.org.uk/big/sct/OKI/ofhs.html

Renfrewshire Family History Society
http://www.geocities.com/renfrewshirefhs

Scottish Association of Family History Societies
http://www.safhs.org.uk

Scottish Clan and Family Associations
http://clan-maccallum-malcolm.3acres.org/ScotClanFamily.html

Scottish Genealogy Society
http://www.scotsgenealogy.com

Shetland Family History Society
http://www.users.zetnet.co.uk/shetland-fhs

Society of Genealogists
http://www.sog.org.uk

Tay Valley Family History Society
http://www.tayvalleyfhs.org.uk/index.html

Troon @ Ayrshire Family History Society
http://www.troonayrshirefhs.org.uk

SOURCE GUIDES

Familia
http://www.earl.org.uk/familia/preamb1.html

Familyrecords.gov. Aims to give easy access to information and links to the main UK family history sites on the Web.
http://www.familyrecords.gov.uk

GENUKI home page
http://www.genuki.org.uk

Irish ancestors. Details of sources for Irish genealogy, including some primary sources.
http://scripts.ireland.com/ancestor/

Online Genealogical Database Index. Based in the USA Claims to have links to all known genealogical databases searchable through the WWW. These are mainly databases of particular families rather than of original sources and tend to be named after their author, which may not be a good indicator of the data they include.
http://www.gentree.com/gentree.html

SURNAME LISTS

GENUKI Surname Lists
http://www.genuki.org.uk/indexes/SurnamesLists.html

RootsWeb Surname List (RSL) – largest surname list. US-based.
http://rsl.rootsweb.com

APPENDIX 4

USEFUL ADDRESSES

NATIONAL RECORDS

National records
Court of the Lord Lyon
HM New Register House,
Edinburgh EH1 3YT
Tel: 0131 556 7255

General Register Office for Scotland
New Register House,
Edinburgh EH1 3YT
Tel: 0131 334 0380

National Archives of Scotland
HM General Register House,
Edinburgh EH1 3YY
Tel: 0131 535 1314

National Library of Scotland
George IV Bridge,
Edinburgh EH1 1EW
Tel: 0131 226 4531

National Register of Archives for Scotland
HM General Register House,
Edinburgh EH1 3YY
Tel: 0131 535 1405

Registers of Scotland
Customer Service Centres
　Erskine House,
　68 Queen Street,
　Edinburgh EH2 4NF
　Tel: 0845 607 0161

　5 George Square,
　Glasgow G2 1DY
　Tel: 0845 607 0164

Registrar of Births, Deaths and Marriages
89 Commercial Street,
Dundee DD1 2AF
Tel: 01382 435222

Registrar of Births, Deaths and Marriages
22 Park Circus,
Glasgow G3
Tel: 0141 287 8350

Scottish Jewish Archives Centre
129 Hill Street,
Glasgow G3 6UB
Tel: 0141 332 4911

West Register House
Charlotte Square,
Edinburgh EH2 4DP

CHURCH OF JESUS CHRIST OF LATTER-DAY SAINTS FAMILY HISTORY CENTRES

Aberdeen
North Anderson Drive,
Aberdeen
Tel: 01224 692206

Alloa
Grange Road,
Westend Park,
Alloa
Tel: 01259 211148

Alness
Kilmonivaig,
Seafield,
Portmahomack,
Ross-shire.
Tel: 01862 871631

Dumfries
36 Edinburgh Road,
Albanybank,
Dumfries.
Tel: 01387 254865

Dundee
Bingham Terrace,
Dundee
Tel: 01382 451247

Edinburgh
30A Colinton Road,
Edinburgh
Tel: 0131 337 3049

Elgin
Pansport Road,
Elgin,
Morayshire
Tel: 01343 546429

Glasgow
35 Julian Avenue,
Glasgow
Tel: 0141 357 1024

Inverness
LDS Chapel,
13 Ness Walk,
Inverness
Tel: 01463 231220

Kilmarnock
1 Whatriggs Road,
Kilmarnock,
Ayrshire
Tel: 01563 526560

Kirkcaldy
Winifred Crescent,
Forth Park,
Kirkcaldy,
Fife
Tel: 01592 640041

Lerwick
South Road,
Lerwick,
Shetland Islands
Tel: 01595 695732

Paisley
Glenburn Road,
Paisley,
Renfrewshire
Tel: 0141 884 2780

Stornoway
Newton Street,
Stornoway,
Western Isles
Tel: 01851 870972

LOCAL COLLECTIONS

Aberdeen City Council
Aberdeen City Archives,
Town House,
Broad Street,
Aberdeen AB10 1AQ
Tel: 01224 522513

Aberdeenshire Council
Aberdeenshire Council Archives,
Old Aberdeen House,
Dunbar Street,
Aberdeen AB22 8YP
Tel: 01224 481775

Angus Council
Angus Archives,
Montrose Library,
214 High Street,
Montrose DD10 8PH
Tel: 01674 671415

Argyll and Bute Council
Argyll and Bute Council Archives,
Manse Brae,
Lochgilphead,
Argyll PA31 8QU
Tel: 01546 604120

Ayrshire Councils
Ayrshire Archives Centre,
Craigie Estate,
Ayr KA8 0SS
Tel: 01292 287584

Borders Council
Scottish Borders Archive and Local History Centre,
St Mary's Mill,
Selkirk TD7 5EU
Tel: 01750 20842 (extn 26)

Clackmannanshire Council
Clackmannanshire Council Archives,
Library Services,
26–28 Drysdale Street,
Alloa FK10 1JL
Tel: 01259 722262

Dumfries and Galloway Council
Dumfries and Galloway Archives,
33 Burns Street,
Dumfries DG1 2PS
Tel: 01387 269254

Dundee City Council
Dundee City Archive and Record Centre,
Support Services,
21 City Square,
Dundee DD1 3BY
Tel: 01382 434494

Search Room
1 Shore Terrace,
Dundee
Tel: 01382 434494

East Dunbartonshire Council
Information and Archives,
William Patrick Library,
2–4 West High Street,
Kirkintilloch G66 1AD
Tel: 0141 776 8090

Edinburgh City Council
Edinburgh City Archives,
City Chambers,
High Street,
Edinburgh EH1 1YJ
Tel: 0131 529 4616

Edinburgh Room
Edinburgh City Libraries,
Central Library,
George IV Bridge,
Edinburgh EH1 1EG
Tel: 0131 225 5584

Falkirk Council
Falkirk Archives,
Callendar House Museum and History Research Centre,
Falkirk FK1 1YR.
Tel: 01324 503770

Fife Council
Fife Council Archive Centre,
Carleton House,
Balgonie Road,
Markinch,
Fife KY7 6AH.
Tel: 01592 413256

Glasgow Archdiocese (Roman Catholic)
Archdiocesan Archive,
Archdiocese of Glasgow Curial Offices,
196 Clyde Street,
Glasgow G1 4JY
Tel: 0141 226 5898 (extn 154)

Glasgow City Council
Glasgow City Archives,
Mitchell Library,
201 North Street,
Glasgow G3 7DN
Tel: 0141 287 2910

History and Glasgow Room
Mitchell Library,
201 North Street,
Glasgow G3 7DN
Tel: 0141 287 2937

Highland Council
Highland Council Archive,
Inverness Library,
Farraline Park,
Inverness IV1 1NH
Tel: 01463 220330

North Highland Archive
Wick Library,
Sinclair Terrace,
Wick,
Caithness KW1 5AB
Tel: 01955 606432

Midlothian Council
Midlothian Council Archives,
Library Headquarters,
2 Clerk Street,
Loanhead,
Midlothian EH20 9DR
Tel: 0131 440 2210

Moray Council
Local Heritage Centre,
Grant Lodge,
Cooper Park,
Elgin,
Moray IV30 1HS
Tel: 01343 563413

North Lanarkshire Council
North Lanarkshire Archives,
10 Kelvin Road,
Lenziemill,
Cumbernauld G67 2BD
Tel: 01236 737114

Orkney Council
Orkney Archives,
Orkney Library,
Laing Street,
Kirkwall KW15 1NW
Tel: 01856 873166

Perth and Kinross Council
Perth and Kinross Council Archive,
A. K. Bell Library,
2–8 York Place,
Perth PH2 8EP
Tel: 01738 477012

Shetland Council
Shetland Archives,
44 King Harald Street,
Lerwick ZE1 0JX
Tel: 01595 696247

South Lanarkshire Council
South Lanarkshire Archives,
Records Management Unit,
30 Hawbank Road,
College Milton,
East Kilbride G74 5EX
Tel: 01355 239193

Stirling Council
Stirling Council Archives Services,
Unit 6,
Burghmuir Industrial Estate,
Stirling FK7 7PY
Tel: 01786 450745

West Lothian Council
West Lothian Council,
Archives & Records Management Unit,
7 Rutherford Square,
Brucefield Industrial Estate,
Livingston EH54 9BU
Tel: 01506 460020

MEDICAL RECORDS

Dumfries and Galloway Health Board Archives
Easterbrook Hall,
Crichton Royal Hospital,
Dumfries DG1 4TG
Tel: 01387 255301

Greater Glasgow NHS Board Archive
University of Glasgow,
13 Thurso Street,
Glasgow G11 6PE
Tel: 0141 330 5515

Lothian Health Services Archive
University of Edinburgh Library,
George Square,
Edinburgh EH8 9LJ
Tel: 0131 650 3392

Northern Health Services Archives
Aberdeen Royal Infirmary,
Woolmanhill,
Aberdeen AB1 1LD
Tel: 01224 663456 (extn 55562); 01224 663123

Royal College of Physicians and Surgeons of Glasgow
232–242 St Vincent Street,
Glasgow G2 5RJ
Tel: 0141 221 6072

Royal College of Physicians of Edinburgh
9 Queen Street,
Edinburgh EH2 1JQ
Tel: 0131 225 7324

Royal College of Surgeons of Edinburgh
18 Nicolson Street,
Edinburgh EH8 9DW
Tel: 0131 527 1630

OCCUPATIONAL RECORDS

Advocates' Library
Parliament House,
Edinburgh EH1 1RF
Tel: 0131 226 5071

Bank of Scotland
The Archives,
Bank of Scotland,
12 Bankhead Crossway South,
Sighthill,
Edinburgh EH11 4EN
Tel: 0131 529 1288/1305

Royal Bank of Scotland
The Archivist,
Royal Bank of Scotland,
42 St Andrew Square,
Edinburgh EH2 2AD
Tel: 0131 556 7001

Signet Library
Parliament Square,
Edinburgh EH1 1RF
Tel: 0131 225 4923

University of Glasgow Archive Services
13 Thurso Street,
Glasgow G11 6PE
Tel: 0141 330 5516; 0141 339 8855 (extn 4543)

ENGLISH RECORDS

Family Records Centre
1 Myddelton Street,
London EC1R 1UW
Tel: 0181 392 5300

Postal Application Section
General Register Office for England and Wales,
PO Box 2,
Southport,
Merseyside PR8 2JD
Tel: 0151 471 4800

Principal Registry of the Family Division
First Avenue House,
42–49 High Holborn,
London WC1V 6NP
Tel: 020 7947 6000

Public Record Office
Ruskin Avenue,
Kew,
Richmond,
Surrey TW9 4DU
Tel: 0181 876 3444

IRISH RECORDS
REPUBLIC OF IRELAND

The General Register Office
Joyce House,
8–11 Lombard Street East,
Dublin 2
Tel: +353 1 635 4000

Land Registry and Registry of Deeds
King's Inn,
Henrietta Street,
Dublin 1
Tel: +353 1 670 7500

National Archives
Bishop Street,
Dublin 8.
Tel: + 353 1 407 2300

National Library of Ireland
Kildare Street,
Dublin 2
Tel: +353 1 603 0200

Office of the Chief Herald of Ireland
Kildare Street,
Dublin 2
Tel: +353 1 603 0311

NORTHERN IRELAND

General Register Office
Oxford House,
49–55 Chichester Street,
Belfast BT1 4HL
Tel: 028 9025 2021/2/3/4/5

Presbyterian Historical Society
Room 218,
Church House,
Fisherwick Place,
Belfast BT1 6DW
Tel: 028 9025 3936

Public Record Office (Northern Ireland)
66 Balmoral Avenue,
Belfast. BT9 6NY
Tel: 028 9025 5800

SOCIETIES AND ASSOCIATIONS

Aberdeen and North East Scotland Family History Society
The Hon. Secretary,
The Family History Shop,
164 King Street,
Aberdeen AB24 5BD
Tel: 01224 646323

Alloway and Southern Ayrshire Family History Society
c/o Alloway Public Library,
Doonholm Road,
Alloway,
Ayr KA7 4QQ

Anglo-Scottish Family History Society
The Hon. Secretary,
c/o Manchester and Lancashire Family History Society,
Clayton House,
59 Piccadilly,
Manchester M1 2AQ
Tel: 0161 236 9750

Borders Family History Society
The Hon. Membership Secretary,
Caddon Mill,
Clovenfords,
Galashiels TD1 3LZ

Catholic Family History Society
The Hon. Secretary,
45 Gates Green Road,
West Wickham,
Kent BR4 9DE
Tel: 0181 462 4244

Central Scotland Family History Society
The Hon. Secretary,
4 Fir Lane,
Larbert FK5 3LW

Dumfries and Galloway Family History Society
Family History Centre,
9 Glasgow Street,
Dumfries DG2 9AF

East Ayrshire Family History Society
c/o Dick Institute,
Elmbank Avenue,
Kilmarnock KA1 3BU

Federation of Family History Societies
PO Box 2425,
Coventry CV5 6YX

Fife Family History Society
The Hon. Secretary,
'Glenmoriston',
Durie Street,
Leven,
Fife KY8 4HF

Glasgow and West of Scotland Family History Society
The Hon. Secretary,
Unit 5,
22 Mansfield Street,
Glasgow G11 5QP

Guild of One-Name Studies
The Hon. Secretary,
Box G,
14 Charterhouse Buildings,
Goswell Rsoad,
London EC1M 7BA

Highland Family History Society
The Hon. Secretary,
c/o Reference Room,
Public Library,
Farraline Park,
Inverness IV1 1NH

Jewish Genealogical Society of Great Britain
PO Box 13288,
London N3 3WD

Lanarkshire Family History Society
Motherwell Heritage Centre,
High Road,
Motherwell ML1 3HU

Largs and North Ayrshire Family History Society
The Hon. Secretary,
13 Burnside Road,
Largs,
Ayrshire KA30 9BX

Lothians Family History Society
Lasswade High School Centre,
Eskdale Drive,
Bonnyrigg,
Midlothian EH19 2LA

Milngavie Family History Society
Milngavie Community Education Centre,
Milngavie,
Glasgow
Tel: 0141 956 1633

Orkney Family History Society
General Secretary,
Kaimes,
26 Royal Oak Road,
Kirkwall,
Orkney KW15 1RF

Renfrewshire Family History Society
The Secretary,
c/o Paisley Museum and Art Galleries,
High Street,
Paisley PA1 2BA

Scottish Association of Family History Societies
Hon. Secretary,
Alan J. L. MacLeod,
51/3 Mortonhall Road,
Edinburgh EH9 2HN

Scottish Genealogy Society
Library & Family History Centre,
15 Victoria Terrace,
Edinburgh EH1 2JL
Tel: 0131 220 3677

Shetland Family History Society
6 Hillhead,
Lerwick,
Shetland ZE1 0EJ

Society of Genealogists
14 Charterhouse Buildings,
Goswell Road,
London EC1M 7BA
Tel: 0171 251 8799

Tay Valley Family History Society
The Hon.s Secretary,
Family History Research Centre,
179–181 Princes Street,
Dundee DD4 6DQ
Tel: 01382 461845

Troon @ Ayrshire Family History Society
The Hon. Secretary,
c/o MERC,
Troon Public Library,
South Beach,
Troon,
Ayrshire KA10 6AF

SAMPLE FORMS FOR OBTAINING AND RECORDING INFORMATION

Figure A 5.1 Example of a family questionnaire form.

Family Questionnaire Form

(Please give full names & previous surname(s) where appropriate)

You   **Your Husband/Wife (& maiden name)**

Name ....

Date & Place of Birth/Baptism ....

Date & Place of Marriage ....

Date & Place of Death/Burial ....

Occupation ....

Your Children

1 .... 2 .... 3 ....

Name ....

Date & Place of Birth/Baptism ....

Date & Place of Marriage ....

Name of Husband/Wife ....

Date & Place of Death/Burial ....

Occupation ....

Their Children

1 ....

2 ....

3 ....

Your Mother (& maiden name)

....
....
....
....

His Wife (& maiden name)

....
....
....
....

His Wife (& maiden name)

....
....
....
....

Your Father

Name
Date & Place of Birth/Baptism
Date & Place of Marriage
Date & Place of Death/Burial
Occupation

Your FATHER'S Father

Name
Date & Place of Birth/Baptism
Date & Place of Marriage
Date & Place of Death/Burial
Occupation

Your MOTHER'S Father

Name
Date & Place of Birth/Baptism
Date & Place of Marriage
Date & Place of Death/Burial
Occupation

Your current address

Telephone number

Figure A 5.1 Continued.

Family Questionnaire Form

Other Family Members

Do you know any other information about other relatives, such as uncles, aunts, great-uncles, great-aunts, cousins?

1. Full Name .... Relationship...........
   Details ....
   ....
   ....
   ....

2. Full Name .... Relationship...........
   Details ....
   ....
   ....
   ....

3. Full Name .... Relationship...........
   Details ....
   ....
   ....
   ....

Family Traditions

Are there any family traditions or stories which you can recall?

....
....
....
....
....
....
....
....
....
....
....
....
....
....
....

Do you know of the existence of a family Bible? Does it have family details? Where is it?

....
....
....
....

Figure A 5.2 Example of a form for recording birth certificate details.

Birth Certificate Details

First Names:

Surname:

When:

Where:

Father's Name:

Father's Occupation:

Mother's Name:

Date of Marriage (except 1856–61):

Informant:

    Qualification:

    Residence:

When Registered:

Where Registered:

Registrar:

Birth Certificate Details

First Names:

Surname:

When:

Where:

Father's Name:

Father's Occupation:

Mother's Name:

Date of Marriage (except 1856–61):

Informant:

    Qualification:

    Residence:

When Registered:

Where Registered:

Registrar:

Figure A 5.3 Example of a form for recording marriage certificate details.

Marriage Certificate Details:

When, where and how:

Name of GROOM:
    Status:
    Occupation:
    Age:
    Usual Residence:

Name of BRIDE:
    Status:
    Occupation:
    Age:
    Usual Residence:

Father of GROOM:
    Occupation:
    Mother:

Father of BRIDE:
    Occupation:
    Mother:

Minister/Registrar:
When & Where:

Witnesses:

Marriage Certificate Details:

When, where and how:

Name of GROOM:
    Status:
    Occupation:
    Age:
    Usual Residence:

Name of BRIDE:
    Status:
    Occupation:
    Age:
    Usual Residence:

Father of GROOM:
    Occupation:
    Mother:

Father of BRIDE:
    Occupation:
    Mother:

Minister/Registrar:
When & Where:

Witnesses:

Figure A 5.4 Example of a form for recording death certificate details.

Death Certificate Details:

Name:
   Occupation:
   Status:

When:

Where:

Age:

Father's Name:
   Occupation:

Mother's Name
   Maiden Name

Cause of Death
   Duration of Disease:
   Physician:

Informant's Name:
   Qualification:
   Residence:

When Registered:
   Where:
   Registrar

Death Certificate Details:

Name:
   Occupation:
   Status:

When:

Where:

Age:

Father's Name:
   Occupation:

Mother's Name
   Maiden Name

Cause of Death
   Duration of Disease:
   Physician:

Informant's Name:
   Qualification:
   Residence:

When Registered:
   Where:
   Registrar

Figure A 5.5 Example of a form for recording census return details.

Year		Parish		County			Enumerator	

Address	Name	Reln	M or S	Age	Occupation	Where Born

Figure A 5.6 Example of a form for recording IGI details.

IGI Details

Person 1	Person 2	Person 3	Sex	Type	Date	Parish

BIBLIOGRAPHY

GENERAL

Bigwood, Rosemary (1998), *Index to Parishes: With related sheriff courts, commissary courts, and burghs* (n.p).

Bigwood, Rosemary (2001), *Tracing Scottish Ancestors*, Glasgow: HarperCollins.

Blatchford, Robert (ed.) (2001), *The Family and Local History Handbook*, 6th edn, York: The Genealogical Services Directory.

Braham, P. (ed.) (1993), *Using the Past: Audio-cassettes on sources and methods for family and community historians* (6 audio-cassettes with notes), Milton Keynes: The Open University.

Burness, Lawrence R. (1991), *A Scottish Genealogist's Glossary*, Aberdeen: Scottish Association of Family History Societies.

Cairns-Smith-Barth, John Lawrence (1986), *Scottish Family History: A research and source guide with particular emphasis on how to do your research from various sources available within Australia*, vol. 1, Hampton: Sue E. MacBeth Genealogical Books.

Christmas, Brian (1991), *Sources for One-name Studies and for Other Family Historians: A selected list and finding aid*, London: Guild of One-Name Studies.

Cole, Jean A., and Titford, John (2000), *Tracing Your Family Tree: The comprehensive guide to discovering your family history*, 3rd edn, Newbury: Countryside Books.

Colwell, Stella (1997), *Teach Yourself Tracing Your Family History*, London: Hodder & Stoughton.

Colwell, Stella (2001), *Family History: A guide and troubleshooter*. Stroud: Sutton.

Cory, Kathleen B. (1996), *Tracing Your Scottish Ancestry*, 2nd edn, Edinburgh: Polygon.

Diack, H. Lesley (1999), *North East Roots: A guide to sources*. 4th edn, Aberdeen: Aberdeen & North East Scotland Family History Society.

Drake, Michael (ed.) (1994), *Time, Family and Community: Perspectives on family and community history*, Oxford: Blackwell in association with The Open University.

Drake, Michael and Finnegan, Ruth (eds) (1997), *Sources and Methods for Family and Community Historians: A handbook*, 2nd edn, Cambridge: Cambridge University Press in association with The Open University. (*Studying Family and Community History: 19th and 20th centuries*: vol. 4.)

Dumfries & Galloway Family History Society (1995), *Dumfries and Galloway: Some Sources and Places of Interest for Local and Family History*, Dumfries: Dumfries & Galloway Family History Society.

Federation of Family History Societies (1993), *Practice Makes Perfect: A workbook of genealogical exercises*, Birmingham: Federation of Family History Societies.

Finnegan, Ruth and Drake, Michael (eds) (1994), *From Family Tree to Family History*, Cambridge: Cambridge University Press in association with The Open University. (*Studying Family and Community History: 19th and 20th centuries*, vol. 1.)

FitzHugh, Terrick V. H. (1998), *The Dictionary of Genealogy*, 5th edn, London: A. & C. Black.

Fowler, Simon (2001), *Tracing Scottish Ancestors*, Richmond: Public Record Office.

Gandy, Michael (1993), *An Introduction to Planning Research: Shortcuts in family history*, Birmingham: Federation of Family History Societies.

Golby, John (ed.) (1994), *Communities and Families*, Cambridge: Cambridge University Press in association with The Open University. (*Studying Family and Community History: 19th and 20th centuries*, vol. 3.)

Hamilton-Edwards, Gerald (1983a), *In Search of Ancestry*, 4th edn, Chichester: Phillimore.

Hamilton-Edwards, Gerald (1983b), *In Search of Scottish Ancestry*, 2nd edn, Chichester: Phillimore.

Herber, Mark D. (2000), *Ancestral Trails: The complete guide to British genealogy and family history*, 2nd edn, Stroud: Sutton.

Hey, David (2002), *The Oxford Guide to Family History*, Oxford: Oxford University Press.

Irvine, Sherry (1997), *Your Scottish Ancestry: A guide for North Americans*, Salt Lake City: Ancestry.

James, Alwyn (2001), *Scottish Roots: A step-by-step guide for ancestor hunters in Scotland and overseas*, Edinburgh: Luath Press.

Jones, Linda and Milner, Pam (2002), *Genealogist's Guide to Discovering Your Scottish Ancestors*, Cincinnati: Betterway Books.

Kennedy, Ian, Ruthven, Louise, McCulloch, Jean (2001), *Sources for Family History in Ayrshire*, Troon @ Ayrshire Family History Society.

Miller, Susan (1995), *Strathclyde Sources: A guide for family historians*, 2nd edn, Glasgow: Glasgow & West of Scotland Family History Society.

Mills, Elizabeth Shown (1997), *Evidence!: Citation and analysis for the family historian*, Baltimore: Genealogical Publishing Co.

Moody, David (1994), *Scottish Family History*, Baltimore: Genealogical Publishing Co.

Pryce, W. T. R. (ed.) (1994), *From Family History to Community History*,

Cambridge: Cambridge University Press in association with The Open University. (*Studying Family and Community History: 19th and 20th centuries*, vol. 2.)

Sandison, Alexander (1985), *Tracing Ancestors in Shetland*, 3rd edn, London: A. Sandison.

Saul, Pauline (2002), *The Family Historians Enquire Within*, 6th edn, Bury: Federation of Family History Societies,.

Sinclair, Cecil (1997), *Tracing Your Scottish Ancestors: A guide to ancestry research in the Scottish Record Office*, Edinburgh: The Stationery Office.

Steel, D. J. (ed.) (1970), *National Index of Parish Registers: Sources for Scottish Genealogy and Family History*, vol. 12, London: Phillimore.

Tay Valley Family History Society (1988), *Source Book*, Dundee: Tay Valley Family History Society.

Titford, John (2001), *Succeeding in Family History: Helpful hints and time-saving tips*, Newbury: Countryside Books.

Todd, Andrew (2000), *Nuts and Bolts: Family history problem solving through family reconsitution techniques*, 2nd edn, Bury: Allen & Todd.

Wheeler, Meg (1996), *Tracing Your Roots: Locating your ancestors through landscape and history*, (n.p.): Smithmark.

ARCHIVES AND RECORD OFFICES

Bevan, Amanda (ed.) (2002), *Tracing Your Ancestors in the Public Record Office*, 6th edn, Richmond: Public Record Office.

Cole, Jean and Church, Rosemary (1998), *In and Around Record Repositories in Great Britain and Ireland*, 4th edn, Huntingdon: Armstrong, Boon, Marriott Publishing.

Cox, Jane (1997), *New to Kew?: A first-time guide for family historians at the Public Record Office*, Kew: Public Record Office.

Foster, Janet and Sheppard, Julia (eds) (2002), *British Archives: A guide to archive resources in the United Kingdom*, 4th edn, London: Palgrave.

Gibson, Jeremy and Peskett, Pamela (2002), *Record Offices: How to find them*, 9th edn, Bury: Federation of Family History Societies.

Guide to the National Archives of Scotland/Scottish Record Office (1996), Edinburgh: The Stationery Office.

Livingstone, M. (1905), *A Guide to the Public Records of Scotland Deposited in H. M. General Register House*, Edinburgh. Edinburgh: H. M. General Register House.

Mortimer, Ian (ed.) (1999), *Record Repositories in Great Britain*, 11th edn, London: Public Record Office.

Thomson, J. Maitland (1922), *The Public Records of Scotland*, Glasgow: Maclehose, Jackson and Co.

Webster, David W. (1996), *Tracing Scottish Ancestors: Using the computer at New Register House*, Livingston: D. W. Webster.

Wood, Tom (1999), *Using Record Offices for Family Historians*, 2nd edn, Bury: Federation of Family History Societies.

BACKGROUND INFORMATION

Burness, Lawrence R. (1997), *A Scottish Historian's Glossary*, Aberdeen: Scottish Association of Family History Societies.

Chapman, Colin R. (1995), *How Heavy, How Much and How Long?: Weights, money and other measures used by our ancestors*, Dursley: Lochin Pub.

Cheney, C. R. (ed.) (2000), *A Handbook of Dates for Students of English history*, 2nd edn, Cambridge: Cambridge University Press.

Cox, Michael (1999), *Exploring Scottish History: With a directory of resource centres for Scottish local and national history in Scotland*, 2nd edn, Hamilton: Scottish Library Association.

Duncan, A. G. M. (1992), *Green's Glossary of Scottish Legal Terms*, 3rd edn, Edinburgh: W. Green/Sweet & Maxwell.

Gouldesbrough, Peter (1985), *Formulary of Old Scots Legal Documents*. Edinburgh: Stair Society.

Groome, Francis H. (ed.) [1903] (1998), *Ordnance Gazetteer of Scotland*, 6 vols, Bristol: Thoemmes Press.

Index of Scottish Placenames (1981), Edinburgh: HMSO.

Mitchell, B. R. (1988), *British Historical Statistics*, Cambridge: Cambridge University Press.

Munby, Lionel (1996), *How Much is That Worth?*, 2nd edn, Chichester: Phillimore.

New Statistical Account of Scotland (1845), 15 vols, Edinburgh: W. Blackwood and Sons. Web version available.

Statistical Account of Scotland (1791–1999), 21 vols, Edinburgh: W. Creech. Web version available.

Steinberg, S. H. (1991), *Historical Tables, 58 BC–AD 1990*, 12th edn, London: Palgrave.

Third Statistical Account of Scotland (1951–), various publishers.

Torrance, D. Richard (1996), *Weights and Measures for the Scottish Family Historian*, Aberdeen: Scottish Association of Family History Societies.

BIBLIOGRAPHIES

Bibliography of Scotland 1976– (1978–), Edinburgh: National Library of Scotland.

Hancock, P. D. (1959), *A Bibliography of Works Relating to Scotland 1916–1950*, 2 vols, Edinburgh: Edinburgh University Press.

Mitchell, Sir Arthur and Cash, C. G. (1917), *A Contribution to the Bibliography of Scottish Topography*, 2 vols, Edinburgh: Scottish History Society.

Moore, Marjorie (1996), *Sources for Scottish Genealogy in the Library of the Society of Genealogists*, London: Society of Genealogists.

Raymond, Stuart A. (1991–4), *British Genealogical Periodicals: A bibliography of their contents*, 4 vols, Birmingham: Federation of Family History Societies.

Raymond, Stuart A. (1999a), *British Genealogical Books in Print*, Bury: Federation of Family History Societies.

Raymond, Stuart A. (1999b), *British Genealogical Microfiche*, Birmingham: Federation of Family History Societies.

Raymond, Stuart A. (2001), *British Family History on CD*, Bury: Federation of Family History Societies.

Scottish Association of Family History Societies (1998), *Members and Publications*, 3rd edn, Scotland: The Association.

BIOGRAPHICAL DICTIONARIES

Anderson, William (1875), *The Scottish Nation*, Edinburgh: A. Fullarton.

Boase, Frederic (1892–1921), *Modern English Biography*, 6 vols, Truro: Netherton and Worth.

British Biographical Archive (1991), microfiche, London: K. G. Saur.

Brown, James D. and Stratton, Stephen Samuel (1897), *British Musical Biography*, Birmingham: Chadfield.

Chambers, Robert (1835), *A Biographical Dictionary of Eminent Scotsmen*, London: Blackie.

Dictionary of National Biography (1885–), various publishers.

Dictionary of National Biography on CD-ROM (1995), Oxford: Oxford University Press.

Eyre-Todd, George (1909), *Who's Who in Glasgow in 1909*, Glasgow: Gowans & Gray.

Goring, Rosemary (ed.) (1992), *Chambers Scottish Biographical Dictionary*, London: Chambers.

Jeremy, D. and Shaw, C. (eds) (1984–6), *Dictionary of Business Biography*, 5 vols, London: Butterworth.

Saville, J. and Bellamy, J. (1992), *Dictionary of Labour Biography*, 9 vols, London: Macmillan.

Slaven, Anthony and Checkland, Sydney (eds) (1990), *Dictionary of Scottish Business Biography, 1860–1960*, 2 vols, Aberdeen: Aberdeen University Press.

Who Was Who (1897–), London: A. & C. Black.

Who's Who (1849–), London: A. & C. Black. Biographical information included from 1897.

Who's Who (1998), CD-ROM, London: A. & C. Black. Covers 1897–1998.

CENSUS

Escott, Anne (1986), *Census Returns and Old Parochial Registers on Microfilm: A directory of public library holdings in the West of Scotland*, Glasgow: Glasgow District Libraries.

Gibson, Jeremy and Hampson, Elizabeth (2000), *Marriage and Census Indexes for Family Historians*, 8th edn, Bury: Federation of Family History Societies.

Gibson, Jeremy and Hampson, Elizabeth (2001), *Census Returns 1841–1891 in microform: A directory to local holdings in Great Britain; Channel Islands; Isle of Man*, 6th edn, Bury: Federation of Family History Societies.

Gibson, Jeremy and Medlycott, Mervyn (2001), *Local Census Listings, 1522–1930: Holdings in the British Isles*. 3rd edn, Bury: Federation of Family History Societies.

Higgs, Edward (1996), *A Clearer Sense of the Census: The Victorian censuses and historical research*, London: HMSO.

Johnson, Gordon (1997), *Census Records for Scottish Families at Home and Abroad*, 3rd edn, Aberdeen: Aberdeen & North East Scotland Family History Society.

Mills, Dennis and Schurer, Kevin (eds) (1996), *Local Communities in the Victorian Census Enumerators' Books*, Oxford: Leopard's Head Press.

Riggs, Geoff (2001), *Distribution of Surnames in the 1881 British Census*, London: Guild of One-Name Studies.

Ruthven-Murray, Peter (1998), *Scottish Census Indexes: Covering the 1841–1871 civil censuses*, Aberdeen: Scottish Association of Family History Societies.

Using Census Returns (2000), Richmond: Public Record Office, (Public Record Office pocket guides to family history).

CIVIL REGISTRATION

Wood, Tom (2000), *An Introduction to British Civil Registration*, 2nd edn, Bury: Federation of Family History Societies.

CLANS

Adam, Frank (1970), *The Clans, Septs and Regiments of the Scottish Highlands*, 8th edn, Baltimore: Genealogical Publishing Co.

Martine, Roderick (1992), *Scottish Clan and Family Names: Their arms, origins and tartans*, Edinburgh: Mainstream.

COMPUTERS

Bayley, Nigel (1998), *Computer-aided Genealogy: A guide to using computer software for family history*, 2nd edn, Chilmark: S & N Publishing.

Christian, Peter (1999a), *Finding Genealogy on the Internet*, London: D. Hawgood.

Christian, Peter (1999b), *Web Publishing for Genealogy*, 2nd edn, London: D. Hawgood.

Christian, Peter (2003), *The Genealogist's Internet*, 2nd edn., Richmond: The National Archives.

Clayton, John A. (2000), *Internet Ancestry: An introduction to family history and internet research*, Nelson: A. J. Morris.

Crowe, Elizabeth P. (2000), *Genealogy Online: Researching your roots*, London: McGraw-Hill.

Hawgood, David (1997), *Computer Genealogy Update*, London: D. Hawgood.
Hawgood, David (1998), *IGI on Computer: The International Genealogical Index from CD-ROM*, London: D. Hawgood.
Hawgood, David (1999a), *FamilySearch on the Internet*, London: D. Hawgood.
Hawgood, David (1999b), *GEDCOM Data Transfer: Moving your family tree*. 3rd edn, London: D. Hawgood.
Hawgood, David (1999c), *Internet for Genealogy*, 2nd edn, London: D. Hawgood.
Hawgood, David (2000), *GENUKI: UK and Ireland Genealogy on the Internet*, London: D. Hawgood.
Helm, Matthew and Helm, April Leigh (2001), *Genealogy Online for Dummies*, 3rd edn, Foster City, CA: IDG Books Worldwide.
Howells, Cyndi (1997), *Netting Your Ancestors: Genealogical research on the Internet*, Baltimore: Genealogical Publishing Co.
Kovacs, Diane (2001), *Genealogical Research on the Web*, London: Neal-Schumann.
Lawton, Guy (1994), *Spreadsheet Family Trees*, London: D. Hawgood.
McClure, Rhonda (2000), *The Complete Idiot's Guide to Online Genealogy*, Indianapolis: Alpha Books.
Peacock, Caroline (2000), *Genealogy*, London: The Good Web Guide Ltd.
Renick, Barbara and Wilson, Richard S. (1998), *The Internet for Genealogists: A beginner's guide*, 4th edn, Cincinnati: Betterway Books.
Schaefer, Christina K. (1999), *Instant Information on the Internet!: A genealogist's no-frills guide to the British Isles*, Baltimore: Genealogical Publishing Co.
Tippey, David (1996), *Genealogy on the Macintosh*, London: D. Hawgood.

CURRENT RESEARCH

British Isles genealogical register (Big-R) (2000), Bury: Federation of Family History Societies.
Johnson, Keith A. and Sainty, Malcolm R. (eds) (2001), *Genealogical Research Directory: National & international*, 3rd millennium edn, Sydney: Johnson and Malcolm.
International Genealogical Directory (1971–), Sussex: Pinhorns.
National Genealogical Directory (1979–), Sussex: Michael J. Burchall and Judy Warren.
Register of one-name studies 2001 (2001), 17th edn, Burton-on-Trent: Guild of One-Name Studies.

EDUCATION

Chapman, Colin R. (1992), *The Growth of British Education and its Records*, 2nd edn, Dursley: Lochin Publishing.

Chapman, Colin R. (1999), *Basic Facts About Using Education Records*, Bury: Federation of Family History Societies.

Craigie, James (1970), *A Bibliography of Scottish Education Before 1872*, London: University of London Press.

Craigie, James (1974), *A Bibliography of Scottish Education 1872–1972*, London: University of London Press.

Harrison, Margaret (1994), *Scottish Education Bibliography 1970–1990 on CD-ROM*, Glasgow: University of Strathclyde, Jordanhill Library.

Jacobs, Phyllis M. (1964), *Registers of the Universities, Colleges and Schools of Great Britain and Ireland*, London: Athlone Press.

ABERDEEN UNIVERSITY

Anderson, Peter John (ed.) (1893), *Officers and Graduates of University and King's College, Aberdeen, 1495–1860*, Aberdeen: New Spalding Club.

Anderson, Peter John (ed.) (1900), *Roll of Alumni in Arts of the University and King's College of Aberdeen, 1596–1860*, Aberdeen: University of Aberdeen.

Anderson, Peter John and Johnstone, James Fowler Kellas (eds) (1889–98), *Fasti Academiae Mariscallanae Aberdonensis, 1593–1860*, 3 vols, Aberdeen: New Spalding Club.

Donald, L. and MacDonald, W. S. (eds) (1982), *Roll of the Graduates of the University of Aberdeen 1956–1970, with supplement 1860–1955*, Aberdeen: Aberdeen University Press.

Johnston, William (ed.) (1906), *Roll of the Graduates of the University of Aberdeen, 1860–1900*, Aberdeen: University of Aberdeen.

Mackintosh, John (1960), *Roll of the Graduates of the University of Aberdeen 1926–1955, with supplement 1860–1925*, Aberdeen: University of Aberdeen.

Watt, Theodore (1935), *Roll of the Graduates of the University of Aberdeen 1901–1925, with supplement 1860–1900*, Aberdeen: Aberdeen University Press.

GLASGOW UNIVERSITY

Addison, W. Innes (ed.) (1898), *A Roll of the Graduates of the University of Glasgow from 1727 to 1897*, Glasgow: J. Maclehose and Sons.

Addison, W. Innes (ed.) (1913), *The Matriculation Albums of the University of Glasgow from 1728 to 1858*, Glasgow: J. Maclehose and Sons.

ST ANDREWS UNIVERSITY

Anderson, James Maitland (ed.) (1905), *The Matriculation Roll of the University of St. Andrews, 1747–1897*, Edinburgh: W. Blackwood and Sons.

Anderson, James Maitland (ed.) (1926), *Early Records of the University of St. Andrews: The graduate roll 1413–1579 and the matriculation roll 1473–1579*, Edinburgh: Scottish History Society.

EMIGRATION AND IMMIGRATION

British Overseas: A guide to records of their births, baptisms, marriages, deaths and burials, available in the United Kingdom (1994), 3rd edn, London: Guildhall Library.

Dictionary of Scottish Emigrants into England and Wales (1984–92), 5 vols, Manchester: Anglo-Scottish Family History Society, then Manchester & Lancashire Family History Society.

Dobson, David, Various publications. See Web site at http://www.users.zetnet.co.uk/dobson.genealogy.

Filby, P. William and Nemeh, Katherine H. (2000–), *Passenger and Immigration Lists Index: A guide to published records of more than 3,430,000 immigrants who came to the New World between the sixteenth and the mid-twentieth centuries*, 3 vols and later supplements, Detroit: Gale Group.

Kershaw, Roger (2002), *Emigrants and Expats: A guide to sources on UK emigration and residents overseas*, Richmond: Public Record Office.

Kershaw, Roger and Pearsall, Mark (2000), *Immigrants and Aliens: A guide to sources on UK immigration and citizenship*, Kew: Public Record Office.

Lawson, James (1990), *The Emigrant Scots: An inventory of extant ships manifests (passenger lists) in Canadian archives for ships travelling from Scotland to Canada before 1900*, Aberdeen: Aberdeen & North East Scotland Family History Society.

Num, Cora (1999), *How to Find Shipping and Immigration Records in Australia*, 4th edn, Pearce, ACT: Cora Num.

Peoples of Scotland: A multi-cultural history: historical background, list of documents, extracts and facsimiles (1994), Edinburgh: Scottish Record Office.

Whyte, Donald (1986), *Dictionary of Scottish Emigrants to the USA*, 2 vols, Baltimore: Magna Carta Books Co.

Whyte, Donald (1995a), *Dictionary of Scottish Emigrants to Canada before Confederation*, 2 vols, Toronto: Ontario Genealogical Society.

Whyte, Donald (1995b), *The Scots Overseas: A selected bibliography*, Aberdeen: Scottish Association of Family History Societies.

Wilkins, Frances (1993), *Family Histories in Scottish Customs Records*, Kidderminster: Wyre Forest Press.

GENETICS

Daus, Carol (1999), *Past Imperfect: How tracing your family medical history can save your life*, Santa Monica: Santa Monica Press.

Gormley, Myra Vanderpool (1998), *Family Diseases: Are you at risk?*, Baltimore: Clearfield.

Savin, Alan (2000), *DNA for Family Historians*, Maidenhead: Alan Savin.

Sykes, Bryan (ed.) (1999), *The Human Inheritance: Genes, language, and evolution*, Oxford: Oxford University Press.

Sykes, Bryan (2001), *The Seven Daughters of Eve*, London: Bantam.

HANDWRITING

Hector, L. C. (1980), *The Handwriting of English Documents*, 2nd edn, Dorking: Kohler and Coombes.

Johnson, Charles and Jenkinson, Hilary (1915), *English Court Hand, AD 1066 to 1500*, 2 vols, Oxford: Clarendon Press.

Scottish Handwriting 1500–1700: A self-help pack (1994), Edinburgh: Scottish Record Office.

Simpson, Grant G. (1998), *Scottish Handwriting 1150–1650: An introduction to the reading of documents*, East Linton: Tuckwell Press.

HERALDRY

Boutell, Charles (1988), *Boutell's Heraldry*, London: Frederick Warne.

Burnett, Charles J. and Dennis, Mark D. (1997), *Scotland's Heraldic Heritage: The Lion rejoicing*, Edinburgh: The Stationery Office.

Friar, Stephen (1996), *Heraldry for the Local Historian and Genealogist*, Stroud: Sutton.

Innes of Learney, Sir Thomas (1978), *Scots Heraldry*, London: Johnston and Bacon.

Moncrieffe of that Ilk, Sir Iain and Pottinger, Don (1978), *Simple Heraldry*, 2nd edn, Edinburgh: Bartholomew.

Paul, Sir James Balfour (1977), *An Ordinary of Arms Contained in the Public Register of All Arms and Bearings (1672–1902)*, with vol. 2 (1903–73) by David Reid of Robertland and Vivien Wilson, Edinburgh: Lyon Office.

Swinnerton, Iain (1995), *Basic Facts about Heraldry for Family Historians*, Birmingham: Federation of Family History Societies.

HISTORICAL DEMOGRAPHY

Flinn, Michael (1977), *Scottish Population History from the 17th Century to the 1930s*, Cambridge: Cambridge University Press.

Fraser, W. Hamish and Maver, Irene (1996), *Glasgow, vol. II: 1830 to 1912*, Manchester: Manchester University Press.

Macdonald, D. F. (1978), *Scotland's Shifting Population, 1770–1850*, Philadelphia: Porcupine Press.

Pooley, Colin and Turnbull, Jean (1998), *Migration and Mobility in Britain Since the Eighteenth Century*, London: UCL Press.

Schurer, Kevin and Arkell, Tom (1992), *Surveying the People*, Oxford: Leopard's Head.

Wrigley, E. A. (ed.) (1966), *An Introduction to English Historical Demography*, London: Weidenfeld & Nicolson.

Wrigley, E. A. (1973), *Identifying People in the Past*, London: Arnold.

IGI (INTERNATIONAL GENEALOGICAL INDEX) AND FAMILY SEARCH (CD-ROM VERSION OF IGI)

Hawgood, David (1998), *IGI on Computer: The International Genealogical Index from CD-ROM*, London: D. Hawgood.

Hawgood, David (1999), *FamilySearch on the Internet*, London: D. Hawgood.

INDEXES OF FAMILY HISTORIES

Barrow, Geoffrey B. (1977), *The Genealogist's Guide: An index to printed British pedigrees and family histories, 1950–1975*, London: Research Publishing Co.

Ferguson, Joan P. S. (1986), *Scottish Family Histories*, Edinburgh: National Library of Scotland.

Grant, Francis J. (1908), *Index to Genealogies, Birthbriefs and Funeral Escutcheons Recorded in the Lyon Office*, Edinburgh: Scottish Record Society.

Kaminkow, Marion J. (1967), *Genealogical Manuscripts in British libraries: A descriptive guide*, Baltimore: Magna Charta Book Co.

Marshall, George W. [1903] (1998), *The Genealogist's Guide*, Baltimore: Clearfield.

Stuart, Margaret [1930] (1994), *Scottish Family History: A guide to works of reference on the history and genealogy of Scottish families*, Baltimore: Genealogical Publishing Co. (With an essay on how to write the history of a family, by Sir James Balfour Paul.)

Whitmore, J. B. (1953), *A Genealogical Guide: An index to British pedigrees in continuation of Marshall's Genealogist's guide, 1903*, London: Walford Bros.

IRISH FAMILY HISTORY

Begley, Donal F. (1984), *Handbook on Irish Genealogy: How to trace your ancestors and relatives in Ireland*, 6th edn, Dublin: Heraldic Artists.

Fowler, Simon (2001), *Tracing Irish Ancestors*, Kew: Public Record Office.

Grenham, John (1999), *Tracing Your Irish Ancestors: The complete guide*, 2nd edn, Dublin: Gill & Macmillan.

Griffith, Richard (1850–61), *General Valuation of Ireland*, Dublin: Her Majesty's Stationery Office.

Index of Irish Wills 1484–1858 (1999), CD-ROM, Dublin: Eneclann.

JOURNALS

Ancestors, the family history magazine of the Public Record Office, Richmond: Public Record Office, 2001– .

Computers in Genealogy, London: Society of Genealogists, 1982– .

Family History, Canterbury: Institute of Heraldic and Genealogical Studies, 1962– .

Family History Monthly, London: Diamond Publishing Group, 1995– .

Family History News and Digest, Birmingham: Federation of Family History Societies, 1977– .

Family Tree Magazine, Huntingdon: ABM Publishing, 1984– .

Genealogical Computing, Salt Lake City, UT: Ancestry Inc., 1981– .

Genealogical Periodical Annual Index, Bowie, MD: Heritage Books, 1962– . e-book editions available for 1992–2000, see publisher's Web site.

Genealogists Magazine, London: Society of Genealogists, 1925– .

Journal of Family History: Studies in family, kinship and demography, Thousand Oaks, CA: Sage, 1976– .

Periodical Source Index (PERSI), CD-ROM, Fort Wayne, IN: Allen County Public Library. (Subject index to genealogy and local history periodicals written in English and French [Canada] mainly since 1800, although some earlier material is included. Largest index of its type, with almost 5,000 periodicals having been indexed. Also available to Ancestry.com subscribers.)

Practical Family History, Huntingdon: ABM Publishing, 1997– .

Raymond, Stuart A. (1991–4), *British Genealogical Periodicals: A bibliography of their contents*, 4 vols, Birmingham: Federation of Family History Societies: Exeter: S. A. & M. J. Raymond.

Scottish Genealogist, Edinburgh: Scottish Genealogy Society, 1954– .

Your Family Tree, Bath: Future Publishing, 2003– .

LATIN

Gandy, Michael (1995), *Basic Approach to Latin for Family Historians*, Birmingham: Federation of Family History Societies.

McLaughlin, Eve (1999), *Simple Latin for Family Historians*, 6th edn, Aylesbury: Varneys Press.

Martin, Charles Trice [1910] (1997), *The Record Interpreter: A collection of abbreviations, Latin words and names used in English historical manuscripts and records*, Baltimore: Clearfield.

Morris, Janet (1995), *A Latin Glossary for Family Historians*, 2nd edn, Birmingham: Federation of Family History Societies.

Stuart, Denis (1995), *Latin for Local and Family Historians: A beginner's guide*, Chichester: Phillimore.

Your Family Tree, Bath: Future Publishing, 2003– .

NEWSPAPERS

Chapman, Colin R. (1993), *An Introduction to Using Newspapers and Periodicals*, Birmingham: Federation of Family History Societies.

Collins, Audrey (2001), *Using Colindale and Other Newspaper Repositories*, Bury: Federation of Family History Societies.

Ferguson, Joan P. S. (1984), *Directory of Scottish Newspapers*, Edinburgh: National Library of Scotland.

Glasgow Herald Index 1906–84, available in the Mitchell Library, Glasgow.

McLaughlin, Eve (2000), *Family History from Newspapers*, 3rd edn, London: Society of Genealogists.

NONCONFORMISTS

Baptie, Diane (2000), *Records of Baptisms, Marriages and Deaths in the Scottish Secession Churches* (including lists of members), Aberdeen: Scottish Association of Family History Societies.

Breed, G. R. (1995), *My Ancestors were Baptists: How can I find out more about them?*, 3rd edn, London: Society of Genealogists.

Gandy, Michael (1993a), *Catholic Missions and Registers 1700–1880*, Volume 6: Scotland, London: M. Gandy.

Gandy, Michael (1993b), *Catholic Parishes in England, Wales and Scotland: An atlas*, London: M. Gandy.

Gandy, Michael (1996), *Catholic Family History: A bibliography for Scotland*, London: M. Gandy.

Leary, William (1999), *My Ancestors were Methodists: How can I find out more about them?*, London: Society of Genealogists.

Logan, Roger (2000), *An Introduction to Friendly Society Records*, Bury: Federation of Family History Societies.

Milligan, Edward H. (1999), *My Ancestors were Quakers: How can I find out more about them?*, 2nd edn, London: Society of Genealogists.

Mordy, Isobel and Gandy, Michael (1996), *My Ancestors were Jewish: How can I find out more about them?*, 2nd edn, London: Society of Genealogists.

Ruston, Alan (2001), *My Ancestors were English Presbyterians or Unitarians: How can I find out more about them?* 2nd edn, London: Society of Genealogists.

Steel, D. J. (ed.) (1972), *National Index of Parish Registers, volume 2: Sources for nonconformist genealogy and family history*, London: Society of Genealogists.

Steel, D. J. and Samuel, E. R. (eds) (1973), *National Index of Parish Registers, volume 3: Sources for Roman Catholic and Jewish genealogy and family history*, London: Society of Genealogists.

Wenzerul, Rosemary (2001), *A Beginner's Guide to Jewish Genealogy in Great Britain*, 2nd edn, London: Jewish Genealogical Society of Great Britain.

Wiggins, Ray (1999), *My Ancestors were in the Salvation Army: How can I find out more about them?*, 2nd edn, London: Society of Genealogists.

OCCUPATIONS

Culling, Joyce (1999), *An Introduction to Occupations: A preliminary list*, 2nd edn, Birmingham: Federation of Family History Societies.

Raymond, Stuart A. (1996), *Occupational Sources for Genealogists: A bibliography*, 2nd edn, Birmingham: Federation of Family History Societies.

Torrance, D. Richard (1998), *Scottish Trades, Professions, Vital Records & Directories: A selected bibliography*, Aberdeen: Scottish Association of Family History Societies.

Waters, Colin (1999), *A Dictionary of Old Trades, Titles and Occupations*, Newbury: Countryside Books.

ARMED FORCES

Army

'Army List', 1740, 1754– (annual), London: War Office.

Dobson, David (1997a), *Scottish Soldiers 1600–1800, Part 1: Registers of testaments*, St Andrews: D. Dobson.

Dobson, David (1997b), *Scottish Soldiers in Colonial America*, Baltimore: Clearfield.

Dobson, David (1997c), *Scottish Soldiers in Continental Europe, Part 1*, St Andrews: D. Dobson.

Fowler, Simon and Spencer, William (1998), *Army Records for Family Historians*, 2nd edn, London: Public Record Office.

Gibson, Jeremy and Dell, Alan (1991), *Tudor and Stuart Muster Rolls: A directory of holdings in the British Isles*, Birmingham: Federation of Family History Societies.

Gibson, Jeremy and Medlycott, Mervyn (2000), *Militia Lists and Musters 1757–1876: A directory of holdings in the British Isles*, 4th edn, Birmingham: Federation of Family History Societies.

Hamilton-Edwards, G. K. S. (1977), *In Search of Army Ancestry*, London: Phillimore.

'Hart's Annual Army List', 1840–1916 (annual), London: J. Murray.

Holding, Norman and Swinnerton, Iain (1999), *The Location of British Army Records 1914–1918*, 4th edn, Bury: Federation of Family History Societies.

Spencer, William (1997), *Records of the Militia and Volunteer Forces 1757–1945*, Richmond: Public Record Office.

Spencer, William (2001), *Army Service Records of the First World War*, 3rd edn, Richmond: Public Record Office.

Swinnerton, Iain (1996), *The British Army: Its history, tradition and records*, Birmingham: Federation of Family History Societies.

Using Army records (2000), Richmond: Public Record Office.

Watts, M. J. and C. T. (1995), *My Ancestor was in the British Army: How can I find out more about him?*, London: Society of Genealogists.

Royal Air Force
'Air Force List', 1919– , London: HMSO.
Spencer, William (2000), *Air Force Records for Family Historians*, Kew: Public Record Office.

Royal Marines
Thomas, Garth (1994), *Records of the Royal Marines*, London: Public Record Office.

Royal Navy
Marshall, John (1823–35), *Royal Naval Biography*, 12 vols, London: Various publishers.
'Navy List', 1814– (annual), London: HMSO.
'New Navy List', 1839–55. London: Various publishers.
O'Byrne, William R. (1849), *A Naval Biographical Dictionary*, London: J. Murray.
Pappalardo, Bruno (2001), *Using Navy Records*, Richmond: Public Record Office.
Rodger, N. A. M. (1998), *Naval Records for Genealogists*, 3rd edn, Richmond: Public Record Office.
'Steel's Navy List', 1782–1817 (annual), London: Steel.

CLERGY

Beckerlegge, O. A. (1968), *United Methodist Ministers and Their Church*, London: Epworth Press.
'Church College in Aberdeen: Free Church College 1843–1900, United Free Church 1900–1929' (1930), complete roll of alumni 1843–1929, Aberdeen: Aberdeen University Press.
Couper, William J. (1925), *The Reformed Presbyterian Church in Scotland, Its Congregations, Ministers and Students*, Edinburgh: United Free Church of Scotland Publication Dept. A Fasti of this Church from 1743–1876.
Ewing, William (1914), *Annals of the Free Church of Scotland 1843–1900*, 2 vols, Edinburgh: T. & T. Clark.
Fasti Ecclesiae Scoticanae: The succession of Ministers in the Church of Scotland from 1560, 9 vols, Edinburgh: Oliver & Boyd.
Lamb, John A. (1956), *The Fasti of the United Free Church of Scotland, 1900–1929*, Edinburgh: Oliver & Boyd.
Macdonald, Donald F. Macleod (1981), *Fasti Ecclesiae Scoticanae, volume 10: Ministers of the church from 1955–1975*, Edinburgh: The Saint Andrew Press.
Macgregor, W. M. (1930), 'A Souvenir of the Union in 1929: with an historical sketch of the United Free Church College, Glasgow', also a complete alumnus roll from 1856–1929, Glasgow: Trinity College Union.

MacKelvie, William (1873), *Annals and Statistics of the United Presbyterian Church*, Edinburgh: Oliphant & Co.

Small, R. (1904), *History of the Congregations of the United Presbyterian Church from 1733–1900*, Edinburgh: David M. Small.

LAWYERS

Grant, Sir Francis J. (ed.) (1944), *The Faculty of Advocates in Scotland 1532–1943 with Genealogical Notes*, Edinburgh: Scottish Record Office.

Henderson, John Alexander (ed.) (1912), *History of the Society of Advocates in Aberdeen*, Aberdeen: New Spalding Club. Includes a list of members 1549–1911 with biographical notes.

History of the Society of Writers to her Majesty's Signet (1890), with list of members from 1594 to 1890, Edinburgh: Society of Writers to her Majesty's Signet.

'Index juridicus: The Scottish law list 1846–1961', Edinburgh: A. & C. Black.

'Register of the Society of Writers to the Signet' (1983), Edinburgh: Clark, Constable. Details of members from the fifteenth century to the 1980s.

MEDICAL AND RELATED PROFESSIONS

Amsden, Peter C. (1999), *The Medical Professions and Their Archives*, Oban: ASAT Productions.

Bourne, Susan and Chicken, Andrew H. (1994), *Records of the Medical Professions: A practical guide for the family historian*, (n.p.): S. Bourne and A. H. Chicken.

'Dentists' Register', 1879– (annual) London: various publishers.

'London and Provincial Medical Directory', 1861–69, London: J. Churchill.

'Medical Directory', 1845– (annual), London: Churchill Livingstone.

'Medical Directory for Scotland', 1852–60. London: J. Churchill.

'Medical Register', 1859– (annual), London: General Medical Council.

'Midwives Registers', 1917– (annual).

'The Register of Nurses', 1921– (annual), London: General Nursing Council.

'The Registers of Pharmaceutical Chemists and Chemists and Druggists', 1869– (annual), London: Pharmaceutical Society of Great Britain.

Tough, Alister G. (1993), *Medical Archives of Glasgow and Paisley: A guide to the Greater Glasgow Health Board Archive*, Glasgow: Wellcome Unit for the History of Medicine, University of Glasgow.

MERCHANTS AND TRADESMEN

Anderson, James R. (ed.) (1923–5), *The Burgesses and Guild Brethren of Glasgow, 1573–1750*, Edinburgh: Scottish Record Society.

Anderson, James R. (ed.) (1931–5), *The Burgesses and Guild Brethren of Glasgow, 1751–1846*, Edinburgh: Scottish Record Society.

Watson, Charles B. Boog (ed.) (1926–9), *Roll of Edinburgh Burgesses and Guild-brethren, 1406–1700*, Edinburgh: Scottish Record Society.

Watson, Charles B. Boog (ed.) (1929–30), *Roll of Edinburgh Burgesses and Guild-brethren, 1701–1760*, Edinburgh: Scottish Record Society.

Watson, Charles B. Boog (ed.) (1933), *Roll of Edinburgh Burgesses and Guild-brethren, 1761–1841*, Edinburgh: Scottish Record Society.

OTHER OCCUPATIONS

British Railways Pre-grouping Atlas and Gazetteer (1997), 5th edn, Shepperton: I. Allan.

Cowper, A. S. (ed.) (1997), *SSPCK Schoolmasters 1709–1872*, Edinburgh: Scottish Record Society.

Dobson, David (1992), *Scottish Seafarers of the Seventeenth Century*, Aberdeen: Scottish Association of Family History Societies.

Dobson, David (1995), *Scottish School Masters of the Seventeenth Century, Part 1*. St Andrews: D. Dobson.

Dobson, David (1996a), *Scottish Maritime Records, 1600–1850: A guide for family historians*, St Andrews: D. Dobson.

Dobson, David (1996b), *Scottish Seafarers of the Eighteenth Century*, Aberdeen: Scottish Association of Family History Societies.

Dobson, David (1997), *Scottish Seafarers: 1800–1830*, St Andrews: D. Dobson.

Edwards, Cliff (2001), *Railway Records: A guide to sources*, Richmond: Public Record Office.

Gibson, Jeremy and Hunter, Judith (2000), *Victuallers' Licences: Records for family and local historians*, 2nd edn, Birmingham: Federation of Family History Societies.

Hogg, Peter L. (1997), *Using Merchant Ship Records for Family Historians*, Birmingham: Federation of Family History Societies.

Loverseed, D. E. (1994), *Gasworker Ancestors: How to find out more about them: a guide to genealogical sources for the British gas industry*, Stockport: DCS.

Richards, Tom (2002), *Was Your Grandfather a Railwayman?: A directory of railway archives for family historians*, 5th edn, Bury: Federation of Family History Societies.

Sherman, Antony (2000), *My Ancestor was a Policeman: How can I find out more about him?*, London: Society of Genealogists.

Watts, M. J. and C. T. (1991), *My Ancestor was a Merchant Seaman: How can I find out more about him?*, London: Society of Genealogists.

OTHER SPECIFIC SOURCES

Amsden, Peter C. (1999), *Basic Approach to Making Contact with Relatives*, Bury: Federation of Family History Societies.

Chapman, Colin R. (1996), *Marriage Laws, Rites, Records and Customs: Was your ancestor really married?*, Dursley: Lochin Publishing.

'Decennial Indexes to the Services of Heirs in Scotland 1700–1859', Edinburgh: HMSO.

Escott, Anne (1986), *Census Returns and Old Parochial Registers on Microfilm: A directory of public library holdings in the West of Scotland*, Glasgow: Glasgow District Libraries.

Floate, Sharon Sillers (1999), *My Ancestors were Gypsies*, London: Society of Genealogists.

Gibbens, Lilian (1997), *An Introduction to Church Registers*, Birmingham: Federation of Family History Societies.

Gibson, Jeremy and Hampson, Elizabeth (2000a), *Marriage and Census Indexes for Family Historians*, 8th edn, Bury: Federation of Family History Societies.

Gibson, Jeremy and Hampson, Elizabeth (2000b), *Specialist indexes for family historians*, 2nd edn, Bury: Federation of Family History Societies.

Gibson, Jeremy and Rogers, Colin (1994), *Poll Books c.1696–1872: A directory to holdings in Great Britain*, 3rd edn, Birmingham: Federation of Family History Societies.

Gibson, Jeremy and Rogers, C. (1996), *Electoral Registers Since 1832: And burgess rolls*, 2nd edn, Birmingham: Federation of Family History Societies.

Inquisitionum ad Capellam Domini Regis retornatarum, 1811–16, 3 vols, London. Summary of retours before 1700.

Lewis, Pat (1999), *My Ancestor was a Freemason*, London: Society of Genealogists.

Litton, Pauline (1996), *Using Baptism Records for Family Historians*, Birmingham: Federation of Family History Societies.

Litton, Pauline and Chapman, Colin (1996), *Basic Facts about Using Marriage Records for Family Historians*, Birmingham: Federation of Family History Societies.

McLaughlin, Eve (1985), *Interviewing Elderly Relatives*, 2nd edn, Plymouth: Federation of Family History Societies.

Parishes, Registers and Registrars of Scotland (1997), Aberdeen: Scottish Association of Family History Societies.

Probert, Eric D. (1994), *Company and Business Records for Family Historians*, Birmingham: Federation of Family History Societies.

Raymond, Stuart A. (2001), *Using Libraries: Workshops for family historians*, Bury: Federation of Family History Societies.

'Retours of Services of Heirs, Covering the Period 1544–1699', CD-ROM, Edinburgh: Scottish Genealogy Society.

'Search guide for adopted people in Scotland', (1997), Birthlink Adoption Counselling Centre at Family Care, London: Stationery Office.

'Services of heirs in Scotland, covering the period 1700–1859', CD-ROM, Edinburgh: Scottish Genealogy Society.

Shaw, Gareth and Tipper, Allison (1997), *British Directories: A bibliography and guide to directories published in England and Wales, 1850–1950 and Scotland, 1773–1950,* 2nd edn, New York: Mansell.

Swinnerton, Iain (1995), *Basic Facts about Sources for Family History in the Home,* Birmingham: Federation of Family History Societies.

Swinnerton, Iain (2001), *Identifying your World War I Soldier from Badges and Photographs,* Bury: Federation of Family History Societies.

Timperley, Loretta R. (1976), *A Directory of Landownership in Scotland, c. 1770,* Edinburgh: Scottish Record Society.

Using Birth, Marriage and Death Records (2000), Richmond: Public Record Office.

PEERAGE AND LANDED GENTRY

Burke's Family Index (1976), London: Burke's Peerage.

Burke's Genealogical and Heraldic History of the Peerage, Baronetage and Knightage (1970), 2 vols, 105th edn, London: Burke's Peerage.

Burke's Landed Gentry (1965), 3 vols, 18th edn, London: Burke's Peerage.

Debrett's Peerage and Baronetage (2000), 146th edn, London: Debrett's Peerage.

Paul, Sir James Balfour (1904–14), *The Scots Peerage,* 9 vols, Edinburgh: D. Douglass. CD-ROM version, Edinburgh: Scottish Genealogy Society.

PHOTOGRAPHS

Linkman, A. (1991), *Caring for your Family Photographs at Home.* Manchester: Documentary Photography Archive.

Oliver, George (1989), *Photographs and Local History,* London: Batsford.

Pols, Robert (1995a), *Dating Old Photographs,* 2nd edn, Birmingham: Federation of Family History Societies.

Pols, Robert (1995b), *Understanding Old Photographs,* Witney: Robert Boyd Publications.

Pols, Robert (1998), *Photography for Family Historians,* Bury: Federation of Family History Societies. This book looks at the taking, processing and storing of pictures for the family archive using today's techniques and technology.

Steel, D. and Taylor, L. (eds) (1984), *Family History in Focus,* Guildford: Lutterworth Press.

RECORDING AND WRITING YOUR FAMILY HISTORY

Bannister, Shala Mills (1994), *Family Treasures: Videotaping your family history: A guide for preserving your family's living history as an heirloom for future generations,* Baltimore: Genealogical Publishing Co.

Calder, A. and Lockwood, V. (1993), *Shooting Video History: A video workshop on video recording for family and community historians, with accompanying notes,* Milton Keynes: The Open University.

Chapman, Philip J. (2000), *An Approach to Illuminating your Family History with Picture Postcards*, Bury: Federation of Family History Societies.

Fitzhugh, Terrick V. H. (1988), *How to Write a Family History: The lives and times of our ancestors*, Sherborne: Alphabooks.

Green H. (1979), *Projecting Family History: A short guide to audio/visual construction*, Plymouth: Federation of Family History Societies.

Hatcher, Patricia Law (1996), *Producing a Quality Family History*, Salt Lake City: Ancestry.

Humphries, S. and Gordon, P. (1993), *Video Memories: Recording your family history*, London: BBC Education.

Kempthorne, Charley (1996), *For All Time: A complete guide to writing your family history*, London: Heinemann.

Lynskey, Marie (1996), *Family Trees: A manual for their design, layout and display*, Chichester: Phillimore.

McLaughlin, Eve (1988), *Laying Out a Pedigree*, Birmingham: Federation of Family History Societies.

Palgrave-Moore, Patrick (1994), *How to record your family tree*, 6th ed. Norwich: Elvery Dowers Publications.

Phillimore, W. P. W. [1888] (1972), *How to Write the History of a Family*, 2nd edn, Detroit: Gale Research Co.

Sagraves, Barbara (1995), *A Preservation Guide: Saving the Past and the Present for the Future*, Salt Lake City: Ancestry.

Swinnerton, Iain (1999), *Basic Approach to Keeping your Family Records*, 2nd edn, Birmingham: Federation of Family History Societies.

Titford, John (1996), *Writing and Publishing your Family History*, Birmingham: Federation of Family History Societies.

STUDY OF GENEALOGY

Hareven, Tamara and Plakans, Andrejs (eds) (1992), *Family History at the Crossroads: A Journal of family history reader*, Princeton: Princeton University Press.

Ryan, Gerald H. and Redstone, Lilian J. (1931), *Timperley of Hintlesham: A study of a Suffolk family*, London: Methuen.

Sayers, S. (1984), 'The psychological significance of genealogy', in Paul Smith (ed.), *Perspectives on Contemporary Legend*, Sheffield: Centre for English Cultural Tradition and Language, University of Sheffield.

Wagner, Sir Anthony (1961), *English Ancestry*, London: Oxford University Press.

Wagner, Sir Anthony (1975), *Pedigree and Progress*, London: Phillimore.

Wagner, Sir Anthony (1983), *English Genealogy*, 3rd edn, Chichester: Phillimore.

SURNAMES

Bardsley, Alan (1996), *First Name Variants*, 2nd edn, Birmingham: Federation of Family History Societies.

Black, George F. [1946] (1996), *The Surnames of Scotland: Their origin, meaning and history*, Edinburgh: Birlinn.

Donaldson, Gordon (1981), *Surnames and ancestry in Scotland*, Scotland: Gordon Donaldson.

Hanks, Patrick and Hodges, Flavia (1997), *A Dictionary of Surnames*, Oxford: Oxford University Press.

McKinley, Richard (1990), *A History of British Surnames*, London: Longman.

Rogers, Colin (1995), *The Surname Detective*, Manchester: Manchester University Press.

Whyte, Donald (2000), *Scottish Surnames*, 2nd edn, Edinburgh: Birlinn.

WILLS

Camp, A. J. (1974), *Wills and their Whereabouts*, 4th edn, Canterbury: Phillimore.

'Commissariot Records', Edinburgh: Scottish Record Society. Indexes to testaments up to 1800.

Gibson, Jeremy (2002), *Probate Jurisdictions: Where to look for wills*, 5th edn, Bury: Federation of Family History Societies.

Gibson, Jeremy (1974), *Wills and Where to Find Them*, London: Phillimore.

Vicars, Arthur (ed.) (1897), *Index to the Prerogative Wills of Ireland, 1536–1810*, Dublin: E. Ponsonby.

INDEX